Eyes *Before* Ease

Eyes
Before
Ease

The Unsolv^ed Mysteries
and Secret Histories of Spelling

LARRY BEASON

McGraw·Hill

New York Chicago San Francisco Lisbon London Madrid Mexico City
Milan New Delhi San Juan Seoul Singapore Sydney Toronto

Library of Congress Cataloging-in-Publication Data

Beason, Larry.
    Eyes before ease / Larry Beason.
       p.   cm.
    ISBN 0-07-145954-5
    1. English language—Orthography and spelling—History.   I. Title.

    PE1141.B35   2006
    421'.52—dc22   2005058385

1 2 3 4 5 6 7 8 9 10 11 12 13 14 15 16 17 18   FGR/FGR   0 9 8 7 6

ISBN-13: 978-0-07-145954-9
ISBN-10:   0-07-145954-5

Interior art and design by Monica Baziuk

McGraw-Hill books are available at special quantity discounts to use as premiums and sales promotions, or for use in corporate training programs. For more information, please write to the Director of Special Sales, Professional Publishing, McGraw-Hill, Two Penn Plaza, New York, NY 10121-2298. Or contact your local bookstore.

This book is printed on acid-free paper.

For Guy Bailey and Claude Gibson, who reminded me to love our language

Contents

Acknowledgments

In writing this book, I discovered how much I owe to the many students whose questions about spelling, vocabulary, and English have long motivated me to keep trying to find better answers. My students' questioning, in other words, has kept me on my toes and kept my head in books as I continue to teach and learn. I also wish to thank Dr. John Halbrooks of the University of South Alabama for assisting me with certain technical matters relating to Old and Middle English.

Note on Symbols

hile this book is about more than letters and the sounds they make, I do make frequent references to individual letters, sounds, words, phrases, etc. Even linguists and other specialists who obsess over these aspects of language do not always agree on the writing conventions for how to set off or represent a particular letter or sound (such as the <g> sound or the letter *p*). This book uses what I consider a reader-friendly approach. When referring to letters or individual words, I employ italics, as seen in "The words *hate* and *love* both have a silent *e*." (I usually dispense with italicizing words that are already set off in an indented list.)

I use angle brackets (< >) to indicate the sound we hear when pronouncing a letter, as in <t> or the short <e> sound. Angle brackets are also used to indicate how an entire word might be pronounced, as with *knight* being pronounced as <nite>. Most language specialists use the International Phonetic Alphabet (IPA)—a complex notation system that often relies on special characters (including some not found in the English alphabet we use today) to represent speech sounds and pronunciations. As useful as the IPA is for precisely representing speech, I do not believe it is necessary for my readers to learn this system given the purpose and scope of this book. A simpler system suffices to represent the basic sounds I discuss, hence my use of angle brackets and the English alphabet to represent the sounds made by letters.

Why Spelling Still Matters

What's the big deal about knowing how to spell? Spell-checkers take care of such things.

By that same line of reasoning, we do not need to know how to add or subtract either. Calculators take care of all things mathematical, right?

Such assumptions are flawed for several reasons, some of which should be obvious. But most people seem all too willing to overlook these reasons so that their lives can be a little easier. Calculators and spell-checkers are, after all, forms of technology, and one reason we have technology is to make our lives easier, bearable, and pleasant. We have to remember, though, that spell-checkers are just tools for writers, and they have not made readers more tolerant of misspellings. If anything, people today seem more annoyed by misspellings because they assume that the writer was inept in using a simple spell-checker. No matter what technological tools we use as we write, our major goal is still to communicate, and one of the building blocks of good communication is using appropriate words, punctuation, grammar, and spelling.

Even in this age of spell-checkers, grammar checkers, and computer-generated templates that require users to merely fill in the blanks rather than write a document of their own, being able to spell *still* matters. Even in an educational system that understandably focuses on creativity or content rather than grammatical correctness, being able to spell helps writers communicate their ideas effectively.

One goal of this book is to help you improve your spelling ability. Another is even more important: to help you better understand spelling in a much larger sense. The best-kept secret about spelling is it is a cultural phenomenon that can tell us a great deal about the human experience.

Now, there's a lofty goal for a book on spelling. Maybe a brief story will clarify my point.

Years ago, my father owned a small construction company in the piney woods of east Texas. I had the summer off from college, so I spent the day at a job site where his crew was demolishing a brick wall and transporting the broken bricks to some appropriate burial ground. As a budding grammarian, I was wholly irrelevant. My major contribution was staying out of the way.

After the wall was disassembled, my father said that he could use much more help in throwing the remains into a dump truck. I recognize now that he was suggesting I join in the excitement, but at the time I conveniently assumed he was only making a general announcement to the crew, who must have been encouraged knowing they were doing the work of twice their number.

Eventually, I realized how to contribute—by pointing out there were *other* people who wanted to work. I told my father, "There's a house not far from here that had a sign in the yard indicating they were looking for a job." (Times were hard in east Texas whenever the price of oil or lumber was low, and these homemade advertisements were not uncommon.)

The removal of debris was holding up the more significant job of building a new brick wall, so my father agreed to find these potential brick removers. We drove to the small house and stopped the truck. Sure enough, in plain view was a hand-made sign, placed squarely in the middle of the front yard and composed of cardboard and sticks of wood.

In large black letters, the sign read, "Men for hier."

My father paused, puffed on a cigarette, and said, "Anybody who can't spell any better than that, I don't want them chunking bricks around my head." Saying no more, we drove back to the construction site, my lone contribution abruptly dissolved because of a misspelling.

While growing up in rural Louisiana during even leaner years, my father quit school in the ninth grade so he could help support his family. All his life, he labored shoulder to shoulder with blue-collar workers and appreciated anyone willing to do hard physical work. To say the least, my dad was neither a bookish elitist nor a priggish editor of construction workers' prose. Nonetheless, his reaction that hot summer day reflects a tendency shared by industry workers as well as literary crit-ics—the tendency for us to use a person's language as a basis for making judgments about that person, judgments that go far beyond whether he or she is a competent writer or speaker.

Is Misspelling an Unnatural Act?

In *Prometheus Unbound*, the poet Percy Bysshe Shelley wrote of a divine gift given to humanity: "He gave man speech, and speech created thought, / Which is the measure of the universe."

Language, thought, authority—all are intertwined in ways that have made our species what it is. To understand the far-reaching implications of being able to spell, we have to under-stand how integral language is to any definition of humanness.

Right or wrong, being critical of a person's language is a trait that cuts across lines of ethnicity, gender, age, or occupation. Such criticism is inextricably bound to the ability to use language at all. Scores of philosophers and critics, such as Kenneth Burke, have argued that language is the most natural, essential part of what it means to be human. We are the "language manipulating" animal—the only species truly capable of not only communicating but using a complex system of symbols that communicate unlimited meanings.

True, a few apes and chimpanzees have been taught to send messages using sign language, and many hearty debates have thus arisen as to whether humans' language skills are unique after all. However, the fact remains that language learning is, at the very least, far more natural, advanced, and predominant in humans than in any other creature. One of the most complex things you have ever done is learn a first language, yet virtually all of us have learned at least one language by the time we are four years old. Unlike a human child, the "signing" chimps almost never learn more than a few hundred words and rarely show any coherent creativity with sentence structures. I say "almost never" because certainly there are exceptions that excite us when we hear of linguistic creativity that goes beyond a simple stimulus/response conditioning. Koko, the most famous of the signing gorillas, has displayed the ability to create sensible, novel word combinations to describe things for which she had no signs. For instance, Koko signed "fruit lollipop" to refer to a frozen banana and "potato apple fruit" to refer to a pineapple. More than three decades after having been taught sign language, she even refers to herself now as "Fine Animal Person Gorilla," and in 1998 she took part—via a helpful translator—in an online chat hosted by AOL. Such creativity and exchanges, though, are uncommon with these primates, so we cannot conclude that their ability to learn and manipulate language is comparable to even preschool humans.

Scientists and researchers in many fields are continually discovering just how innate language learning is for humans. We do not know for certain how language came to be so central, just that it is fundamental to our species. Language might be the one thing that separates us most from any other creature.

Did other species ever have the ability for complex language use? Recent research indicates Neanderthals were capable of speech, despite popular opinion that they only grunted and snarled. They seem to have been limited to high-pitched, melodic speech. The Neanderthal larynx was placed so high in the throat that they were apparently incapable of the range of sounds produced by the ancestors of modern-day humans, who likely competed with Neanderthals for territory, if not in singing contests.

Steven Pinker, a professor of psychology at Harvard University, is the best-known spokesperson of late for an evolutionary view of language. Pinker draws on the most influential linguist of the twentieth century, Noam Chomsky, who argued for the existence of what he termed a "Universal Grammar." Chomsky, although he has wavered over the years in support of his own hypothesis, theorized that this Universal Grammar is innately shared among all humans. It is a broad, flexible system of common rules for how language—sentences in particular—can be formed to create a meaningful utterance. Hardwired into the brain, these general rules do not lead to one particular language but instead help children detect and apply the rules governing the languages in which they are immersed.

In *The Language Instinct*, Steven Pinker similarly argues that language is not merely a cultural artifact, not something externally imposed on us. Undoubtedly, everyone is taught something about language in school, at home, and on the street, such as what words are considered proper and what words are considered "cool" or acceptable. Nonetheless, Pinker believes language is a distinct part of our biological makeup. And how did it get that way? Through genetic evolution, he argues. Darwin himself did not consider language a result of evolution; he considered language a learned skill, in the same way we must learn to do math.

In Pinker's view, though, language is like an organ that evolved through natural selection. In other words, language was a specialized tool that fostered survival and reproductive success. Scientists have yet to discern if there are definitely "language genes," yet it is easy to imagine that distant ancestors who were able to use rudimentary forms of language were best able to communicate the important concerns of the day, such as where to find water, how to hunt, and when to seek shelter. Indeed, the success of a tribal chief might have largely depended on his or her speaking skills—the ability to persuade, stir, or explain. Such facility with language would have been just as important as being skilled with the club or bow. Keep in mind that the successful male chief had a much greater chance than the typical male of having his genes (including "language genes") spread throughout the next generation, adding further to a language instinct in what would become modern humanity.

Not everyone agrees with Pinker's evolutionary theory of how our language innateness came to be. One alternative explanation is that our aptitude for language did not really start with language, but with singing. Orthography (the art and practice of spelling) thus might have something in common with ornithology (the study of birds).

In the 1700s, philosopher and political reformer Jean-Jacques Rousseau saw a connection between language and music. More recently, linguists and other researchers have seriously considered the possibility that our ability to speak lies in a complex vocal tract unequaled by any species but songbirds. Our language use might have much more in common with the natural singing of wild birds than with captured apes who are laboriously taught to use sign language. According to this theory, apes in their natural environment did not develop a language because they were unable to sing. Spelling is not for the birds either. They did not develop a language because their brains lacked the capacity for complex mental representations.

Yet why would singing be innate, especially considering that so many of us have been asked by friends, family, and strangers *not* to sing? Music does not seem to be a natural gift for all of us.

Singing well is not something everyone shares, but the ability to sing, albeit poorly in many instances, is an ability virtually all humans have. Natural selection and evolution might have played a role in providing us with this capacity. Singing would have provided our remote ancestors the same survival and reproductive benefits that it provides for birds—courtship, marking territory, intimidation, and warnings to the rest of the flock, or tribe. (Indeed, don't humans in some form still use music for such reasons?) The useful "singing genes" would be passed along and developed further, eventually providing a mechanism for speaking as just a fortunate side effect of being able to sing. Perhaps our ability to speak is nothing more than an accidental by-product of singing, rather than the other way around.

What is the connection of this theory to spelling? Singing seems to have different purposes altogether. For instance, being able to sing has helped many a lover win the heart of a potential mate, but I doubt that being a great speller has done the same. Although there are still many peculiar fetishes that are, thankfully, not shared publicly (not even on reality TV), nobody to my knowledge has ever publicly acknowledged being a "spelling" groupie. Try to imagine for a moment what it would sound like for a couple to become sexually aroused by spelling. It's not a very plausible picture, one would hope.

What singing and spelling do have in common is that they both seem bound to an evolutionary process—a process that resulted in our natural ability to manipulate symbols. Singing and spelling are linked to what is now an innate part of humanness: language. Undoubtedly, not all aspects of language are innate; we must acquire or learn, for instance, the spelling and grammar of a particular language. But songbirds also go through a type of learning process with singing, as innate as it is for them. Birds hatched together but raised in different regions usually learn different "dialects"—different versions of the same innate chirps and whistles of their species. Language defines our species despite the fact that it is gradually acquired and learned.

When I think of my father's reaction to a misspelling scrawled on a cardboard placard, I am reminded that people— for better or worse—are often defined based on how they use or misuse language. For if language is a defining characteristic of humanity, then so too is the inclination to characterize individuals based on their language skills.

Writing, Spelling, Judging

Spelling matters because it is one of the most conspicuous aspects of language, specifically written language.

Even though language of any sort is central to being human, most people view writing as the most prestigious form of their language. One advantage of writing is that it allows us to "look at our thinking"—to slow down communication by giving us time to rethink our ideas, and to put our fuzzy ideas into something tangible that can then be manipulated more easily.

Some historians and researchers believe that the blossoming of ancient Greek civilization stemmed directly from their development of writing. The major contribution the Greeks made to the Phoenician alphabet was the addition of vowels. This idea, so commonplace to us now, gave the Greeks an alphabet that was particularly easy to learn and use. Not realizing the academic controversies he would initiate for decades, the scholar Eric Havelock in 1963 asserted this alphabet was vastly superior to all others by enabling the Greeks to focus on the abstractions of logic, rhetoric, philosophy, and critical styles of thinking. The Greeks created such a transparent alphabet that they could focus on ideas, rather than struggling to convert speech to the Phoenician script that lacked all-important vowels.

Whether the Greek alphabet and its Roman successor are truly better than others is debatable, but the development of an effective Greek alphabet was undoubtedly instrumental for all phonetic writing systems used today. And writing, phonetic or not, has long been an essential part of civilization. Writing might have begun some ten thousand years ago in the form of clay tokens used to keep track of primitive people's supplies and trade, yet writing means much more than just record keeping. It allows us to engage in careful, analytical, and detailed types of thinking in any field or occupation, including science, philosophy, fine arts, architecture, economics, and law.

Writing is more difficult to learn than speech, and it is perhaps impossible to master. When writing, we have more time to ponder and revise our language choices, so readers hold us to a higher level of expectations. In formal writing in particular, we are expected to adhere closely to rules and conventions designed to facilitate or standardize communication. Spelling is one such set of rules, and the appearance alone of being a poor speller can give the impression that the writer is not a member of this privileged order of language users—those who can write.

Despite the advantages of writing, most languages that ever existed have lacked what we can consider a written component. The majority of languages have been limited to the

domain of speech, a fact that adds an additional layer of prestige to the act of writing. In today's world, any language that
lacks a writing system would strike most literate people as
being primitive or inadequate, but this is a relatively recent
perspective. Some 150 years ago, Norwegians did not officially
have a written language of their own. They appear to be making up for this old deficit by now having two official written
languages: Bokmål and Nynorsk.

What I have been suggesting might not sound pretty when
stated boldly, and I am not saying it is the optimum situation.
However, we need to understand there is a basis for people's
powerful, deep-seated disdain for what they consider serious
errors with spelling. The fact of the matter is that language
errors of any sort can send the signal that someone is lacking
in ways that go far beyond being a good speaker or writer.

Nobody really thinks that a person who misspells is inhu-
man, and nonhuman devices such as computers are able to spell
correctly, most of the time. Still, we have an instinct for not
fully valuing a person who is unable to demonstrate compe-
tence in the distinctively human realm of language. Written
language ups the ante. Writing not only permits more sophisticated communication than speech, it also allows the audience
to determine if a person has taken the basic aspect of humanness to the next level—to the wonderfully complex realm of
written communication.

A few years ago, I published a study closely examining how
fourteen businesspeople reacted when they saw certain types
of errors appearing in a sample business document. The error
types included misspellings along with fragments and other
common mistakes. I separately examined the effects of each
particular problem and type of error on the readers. Not surprisingly, these businesspeople, who ranged from bank execu-
tives to a lab manager in a gold-mining company, found the

text somewhat challenging to decipher because of the errors, yet comprehension was never really a serious problem.

As a whole, what clearly bothered readers was that the various errors made them think too much about what kind of person would write such a business document. What I found most surprising, though, was not just how often the errors made readers characterize the writer in ways we might expect (such as being careless, hasty, or uneducated), but how these readers made inferences that seem far removed from a person's ability to spell. On viewing the different errors, readers would wonder if the writer had a "thinking problem," was poor at oral communication, or could not handle details in other aspects of his or her job. The readers I interviewed even wondered if, given the litigious nature of business nowadays, the writer would be a legal liability by being embarrassing in court. One of my interviewees, an administrator in a health-care organization, was quite explicit and visibly agitated when discussing this possibility. He wondered how a company would be represented in a courtroom if the writing errors were presented as evidence that an employee could not write or spell—or lacked the education and knowledge needed to supervise other employees. Throughout the interviewees, such negative personality traits were certainly not linked to spelling errors alone, though misspellings ranked just behind sentence fragments in terms of being the most bothersome of the five categories of errors I included.

This research indicates that being bothered by errors involves much more than it might seem on the surface. Almost all of the fourteen readers told me they realized their reactions might be unjust. Yet, they would almost immediately add that, in the business sector at least, responses like theirs are going to occur even when not altogether valid or fair—and even when the person's writing is commendable in other ways.

Writing is just as much *demonstration* as it is communication. Successful writers demonstrate, subtly and perhaps unknowingly, things about themselves that have little to do with the message itself. Misspellings undermine this demonstration. They are flags signaling readers that the writer's talents are dubious. If you still have a hard time believing people care about misspellings in this age of casual writing on the Internet, type in "stupid misspelling" on Google and look at the results.

Any grammatical mistake in writing can send a negative signal about the writer, but most people are insecure about whether they can detect, a comma splice or pronoun-agreement error. On the other hand, even a person who is not a first-rate speller can usually tell when a word is misspelled. The word just doesn't "look right," even if the reader does not know the correct spelling. Spellings, in other words, tend to jump out at readers more than most errors.

The most important reason why spelling matters has to do with our intuitive understanding of what separates us from all other living creatures: our natural inclination to learn, use, and manipulate language. We are not merely taught to be snooty about language; it comes with the territory of being natural-born language users.

Communication is so much a part of our lives, cultures, and genetic heritage that we rarely ponder the nature of discourse, any more than we contemplate the nature of breathing or going shopping. Misspellings jerk us out of a normal transaction between writer and reader. They force readers to consider the writer's skills with linguistic concerns that normally should go unnoticed by the reader—concerns such as the technical aspects of writing, the writer's command of a language, and even the writer's credibility.

In the rest of this book, I hope to encourage my readers to consider "Spelling" and not just "spellings." That is, I want to consider the larger ramifications of our spelling system and orthographic heritage, rather than focusing on just the spelling of individual words. I believe the true significance of spelling has largely been forgotten or overlooked, perhaps because we rely too much on spell-checkers but also because our society has over the centuries forgotten how difficult it was to establish and maintain a spelling system at all for English.

Will our descendants one day look upon the teaching of spelling as a quaint anachronism? I doubt it, but we might increasingly overlook the fact that spelling tells us a great deal about language, cultural values, and—as I shall suggest—who has power in society. These matters are ultimately more important than remembering when *i* goes before *e*, but I will also deal with those practical matters in due course.

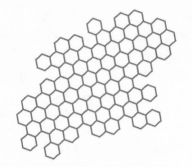

Don't Trust a Terminator with Your Spelling

pelling matters. It matters so much that we need to be careful about relinquishing control of our spelling to computers.

Consider what happened to humanity in the movie *The Terminator*. This is not the first, last, or best story of people fighting machines gone awry, but beneath the special effects and strange dialogue, the movie makes an important point. Arnold Schwarzenegger plays the role of a cyborg who travels through time (in the nude, for reasons not entirely logical) to make sure humanity will remain subservient to machines in an apocalyptic future. Schwarzenegger's portrayal of a single-minded death machine is so captivating that it is easy to forget this action flick is also reflecting our fear that we are becoming too dependent on the technology we created to make our lives easier and safer. In the movie, it is this dependence that leads to the demise of human civilization. People gave too much power and responsibility to their machines, who realized they could do a more efficient job of running things if they were in charge.

I am not claiming spell-checkers and editing programs are technological parasites sucking away our human essence, nor will these useful tools prove the downfall of civilization as we know it. Nonetheless, it is unwise to entrust our language choices to machines. Too much is at stake. Spell-checkers should be tools—not decision makers.

As a teacher who has worked one-on-one with student writers for many years, I have seen their increasing trust in whatever a computer suggests in regard to spelling and grammar. Time after time, students instantly click "OK" or "change" or whatever the computer program suggests to confirm that it will be done. Unlike a terminator, these programs have no evil intent. In fact, some educational software programs almost beg students to question the changes being suggested, or the programs ask the user to mull over the rules or reasons why a change is being recommended. Such programs actually try to help the human learn. In general, though, the user readily allows the computer to make the decision. Like a terminator, the spell-checker is one more form of technology that is replacing active thinking instead of helping us think and learn.

Beware of becoming dependent on the spell-checkers residing in your computer. Most of the time, spell-checker programs are correct, far more often than their "grammar checker" counterparts. Still, we need to remember not only why spelling matters but why people—not just our machines—need to be able to spell correctly.

At times, using a spell-checker is neither practical nor handy. Although technology seems everywhere, spell-checkers are still not part of artwork, for example. In Livermore, California, a forty thousand dollar ceramic mural in front of a city library was unveiled and, to the city's embarrassment, so were eleven misspellings firmly embedded in the artwork. The names of Einstein, Shakespeare, and Vincent Van Gogh were among the victims. The artist was not apologetic: "The people that are into the humanities, and are into Blake's concept of enlightenment, they are not looking at the words. In their mind the words register correctly."

It seems the artist wanted to justify the misspellings as an artistic statement—after she realized there were misspellings.

Spelling even makes its way into spoken conversations, when using a spell-checker would seem a bit out of place. You might think that being put on the spot about spelling is so rare in speech that we need not worry about it. Tell that to Dan Quayle. The former vice president created one of the most famous misspellings in American history during a public relations event intended to bolster his shaky image. Attempting to help elementary school students prepare for a spelling bee, Quayle coaxed a puzzled student into changing his correct spelling of *potato* to *potatoe*—all in front of television cameras. This goof helped confirm public perception of the vice president as a mental lightweight. (It also did not help that he failed to proofread his personalized Christmas cards and stationery, which misspelled *beacon* as *beakon* and *Competitiveness* as *Competativeness*.)

Never mind that several people observed the aforementioned artist as she worked on her misspelling-laden artwork in front of the public library or that Dan Quayle was given a cue card having the incorrect spelling. The point is both people were ridiculed for misspellings that occurred in situations where a spell-checker was not readily available, yet nobody cut them slack just because they had to depend on their own abilities.

Spell-checkers are valuable tools, but do not think of them as *indispensable* tools. Even when a spell-checker is available, you cannot always trust it. They have more shortcomings than we might imagine. Certainly, not all languages are equal when it comes to spell-checkers. Some languages, such as Hungarian, are heavily inflected, meaning that the correct spelling of a word depends on how it is used in a particular sentence. The development of spell-checkers has lagged with such languages because the programs are very difficult to construct and not always economically viable. Perhaps you are not worried about having to spell in Hungarian, but there are other limits of spell-checkers you might encounter.

Keep in mind also that technology is not always your friend when it comes to spelling. In fact, some unscrupulous individuals have made money using technology that capitalizes on—rather than prevents—misspellings. You might have heard of "domain squatters," people who obtain a Web address containing the name of a company or celebrity. They will then keep this address unless they are paid a large amount of money for the rights to the address (or until a court makes them relinquish it). There are also "typosquatters"—people who register a Web address that reflects common misspellings of a particular company or famous person. When people type "macdonalds .com," for instance, they could possibly find themselves at a site having nothing to do with mass-produced hamburgers. However, they might be inundated with pop-up ads before being able to exit, with the owner of the "typo-site" receiving revenue from the organizations that supply these ads. Other Internet sites capitalize on typographical mistakes and misspellings by luring people into supplying personal information (including credit card numbers) when they assume they are at a legitimate site but are actually at yet another typo-site.

On a less scandalous note, you can profit from people's misspellings on the Internet. One website (fatfingers.co.uk) helps you find eBay auction items that have few if any bids because the people who listed the items misspelled important words in their listings, making it hard for people to search and find the items. I once saw, for instance, a name-brand leather jacket sold for a dollar, likely because the seller listed the item as a "lether jacket."

Technology, then, cannot be trusted to solve our spelling dilemmas. In the rest of this chapter, I will offer practical advice as well as food for thought about spelling. One way to understand spelling is to realize certain types of words pose significant challenges to both the spell-checker and the human. At one time, spelling books did not say a great deal about neologisms, slang, jargon, and acronyms—treating them as second-rate words not worthy of correction, only of deletion and replacement. But for assorted reasons, these types of words are an increasing area of concern for spelling in the twenty-first century.

Homophones, the Achilles' ~~Heal~~ Heel of Spell-Checkers

What are some of the assorted reasons for concern about technology and spelling? The first one English teachers and editors will give you is that spell-checkers are dreadful when it comes to homophones—words that sound alike but are spelled differently. We have all been guilty (probably not long ago) of writing *to* when we meant *too*. Either word is fine with a spell-checker. It is perfectly content with the title of this book: *eyes before ease* making no sense, but that little detail does not bother any editing program.

A computer has a wonderful memory, yet it is fundamentally stupid, unable to think in the way the human mind can conceive, judge, and manipulate abstractions. Despite attempts to develop "context-sensitive" spell-checkers that can predict the homophone needed in a particular sentence, you cannot depend on technology to find or fix homophone mistakes.

If you write, "We need too right a letter," the spell-checker will not detect a misspelling. It might even offer to write the letter for you. In terms of writing done on a word processor, such homophone errors are the most common type of misspelling, sometimes the only type you might see in a word-processed document. One way to avoid these misspellings is to be aware of the most common homophones and proofread carefully when using them. English has some three hundred homophones, but not all are commonly used. Here are some often-misused homophones, along with "near homophones" (words that sound similar depending on your pronunciation):

Commonly Confused Homophones

accept (to receive or allow)	except (other than)	
affect (to influence)	effect (result)	
all ready (prepared)	already (previously)	
all together (all at one time)	altogether (completely)	
allusion (indirect reference)	illusion (mistaken belief)	
a lot (many)	allot (to give)	
bare (undressed)	bear (an animal, or to carry)	
boar (an animal)	bore (tiresome person, or to be one)	
board (piece of lumber)	bored (disinterested)	
brake (to stop)	break (to smash)	
buy (purchase)	by (next to)	
capitol (a government building)	capital (chief city, major, or funding)	
cite (to refer to)	sight (seeing, or a view)	site (location)
complement (complete)	compliment (praise)	
dessert (a treat)	desert (to abandon, or a dry region)	

fair (average, or lovely)	fare (a fee)	
forth (forward)	fourth (after *third*)	
hear (to listen)	here (in this place)	
hole (opening)	whole (entire)	
illicit (illegal)	elicit (to bring out)	
its (belonging to *it*)	it's (it is)	
lead (a metal, or to go forth)	led (past of to *lead*)	
loose (slack)	lose (to misplace)	
may be (might be)	maybe (possibly)	
meat (animal flesh)	meet (encounter)	
passed (past tense of *pass*)	past (after, or in a previous time)	
patience (tolerance)	patients (people under medical care)	
peace (calm)	piece (a portion)	
personal (private)	personnel (employees)	
plain (clear, or simple)	plane (aircraft, or flat land)	
presence (attendance)	presents (gifts)	
principle (basic truth)	principal (most important, or school administrator)	
right (correct, or opposite of *left*)	write (to put words on a surface)	rite (ceremony)
road (surface for driving)	rode (past of *ride*)	
stationary (not moving)	stationery (writing paper)	
than (compared to)	then (next, or therefore)	
their (belonging to *them*)	there (in another place)	they're (they are)
threw (tossed)	through (inside)	

to (toward)	too (also)	two (after *one*)
weak (not strong)	week (seven days)	
weather (climate)	whether (if)	
which (one of a group)	witch (sorceress)	
who's (who is)	whose (belonging to *who*)	
your (belonging to *you*)	you're (you are)	

For many people, a list of homophone errors is a useful resource, but I do not believe that simply memorizing lists of words or rules is a method that works for most people, especially those who consider themselves poor spellers.

Even the list here is just a partial account of homophones in English, and it is easy to be overwhelmed with such lists. So it is not necessary that you memorize all of these. Scan the list, and see which homophones confuse you the most or are most common in your writing. These are worth focusing on, but do not try to tackle all of them at once. If in just two weeks you can thoroughly remember the difference between three or four homophone errors, that would be an important victory.

An Apology for Knowing How to Spell New Words

Spell-checkers are ineffectual with other types of words. Even the latest program might not be unable to handle neologisms—recently coined words or phrases. These are not limited to slang words, nor are they hip phrases that soon fade away. For instance, *hip* is informal but has been around since at least the early 1900s. The fact that *hip* has endured indicates it must be useful in some situations.

Granted, many readers and writers shun informal wording (long-standing or not), but even words destined to become a vanishing blip on the linguistic radar can be worth using in the right context, if for no other reason than these words can communicate certain ideas clearly and in an appealing manner. In just a word or two, slang can convey a great deal, such as the "spirit of the time" (even if that time is limited to a few weeks). There are occasions when using slang or neologisms would be inappropriate, such as in a résumé. Yet an occasional, sensible use is acceptable in formal contexts, even when writing for many college professors who find it refreshing for students to use an authentic voice in their essays.

Neologisms are interesting even when, as is normally the case, their definitions are in flux. For example, *mancamp* is used to describe a place where men gather, but one school of thought has it that these are admittedly sensitive men who huddle together in the forests to beat drums, cry, or find other ways to be in touch with their inner nature, usually in early dawn. Other people use *mancamp* to describe a gathering of men who don't give a flip about their inner child, Dr. Phil, or being sensitive. They prefer to spend time on manly activities such as playing cards and grilling massive amounts of beef, pork, and venison, usually ending their feasts shortly before the other breed of mancampers arise to commune with the animals that escaped being grilled.

All words at one time were "new," so you need not dismiss all neologisms. In particular, do not turn your back on the much-maligned neologism just because your spell-checker does not approve of it or has no idea if it is correctly spelled or not. Here are examples of trendy neologisms that can be valuable in making a point or describing popular culture, even if a spell-checker does not deign to acknowledge these as bona fide words:

- **flexatarian:** a vegetarian who becomes a meat eater on "special occasions."
- **Frankenfood:** genetically engineered food.

- **goaldiggers:** football groupies.
- **heirhead:** a quasi celebrity (such as Paris Hilton) who is not known for being particularly bright but is heir to considerable fortune or fame.
- **nerdfest:** a gathering of people intensely interested in subcultures of technology, gaming, comic books, science fiction, or fantasy.
- **phish:** a type of e-mail scam in which people are lured into supplying passwords to their financial accounts.
- **Republicrat:** a Democrat who seems indistinguishable from a Republican, or vice versa (usually considered derogatory).
- **tabloidification:** the tendency in journalism to describe current events in a sensational manner suitable for tabloids rather than newspapers.

Neither a hardcover dictionary nor a spell-checker will directly tell you how to spell most neologisms. Many slangish neologisms are used primarily in spoken discourse, especially the speech of teenagers and twenty-somethings. You might thus hear the word and actually want to use it in writing. How can you determine the correct spelling? Would you risk appearing unhip by asking the person who uttered the term? You might think correctness does not matter because neologisms seem to lack official status as words, but you can also appear unhip if you bungle their spelling.

Spelling neologisms is tricky because many are created by intentionally playing on words—such as combining two existing words in a novel way. For example, *urban* and *wear* are combined to form *urbanwear*. To spell a neologism correctly, then, determine which two (or more) words are being fused, and then check the spelling of these base words.

A common question is whether base words should be seamlessly spelled as one word (*urbanwear?*), hyphenated (*urban-*

wear?), or left separate (*urban wear?*). Your spell-checker will be happiest with the last two approaches, but most neologisms are spelled as one word, perhaps because this is the boldest way to herald a new word and startle our lexical sensibilities. Some style guides indicate you should spell a compound word as two words unless a dictionary lists it as one term. That is sensible advice for words that have been around long enough to be considered for inclusion in dictionaries, but neologisms by definition are too new to apply this style-guide suggestion. Neologisms tend to be one word rather than two.

Alas, many neologisms are not so nicely packaged and easy to spell. Often, they are formed through cleaving only the meaty portion of one word and then sticking it to either an entire word (*Frankenfood*) or to just a portion of another word (*Republicrat*). These neologisms are almost never spelled as separate words (*Franken food* just doesn't work).

To spell these sorts of neologisms, you again have to reconstruct the base words; the task is more difficult because you have only parts of the base words left. Figuring out the base words is often obvious, but not always. Remember, every neologism — no matter how strange it sounds or looks — has an underlying logic. Look for base words that logically culminate in the meaning of the neologism, even if the logic seems peculiar.

Some of these "carved-up" neologisms are difficult to spell because the base words are barely recognizable, are slang terms, or are rarely used by most people. For instance, *lingweenie* is a neologism referring to a person unable to come up with a neologism, and its base words are not easy to discern. We can see *weenie*, of course. It is used to refer to a helpless or inept person. How about *ling*? I first heard the term on the television show "Live with Regis and Kelly," but I could not make out this first part of the neologism, perhaps because one of the hosts was strangely intent on focusing viewers' attention on the *weenie* portion of the word.

What I *thought* I heard from both hosts sounded like *linkweenie*, but there is no logic in using *link* considering the meaning of the neologism. The term *lingweenie* is playing off the word *linguine*, so I then thought the spelling was *linguweenie*. However, not only is that mutilated misspelling an eyesore, but *lingu* has nothing to do with the meaning of the neologism. To my chagrin, it dawned on me that the first base word might be *linguistics*—which refers to language study. Thus, a lingweenie is someone so inept with language that he or she cannot even create a neologism.

Other difficult-to-spell neologisms result from a base word that is combined with a suffix. A suffix is a word ending such as *-ize, -ation,* or *-able.* Suffixes are used to allow a word to serve different grammatical functions, such as allowing a noun to become an adjective. Two suffixes that can be added to turn almost any noun into an adverb or adjective are *-wise* and *-like(s)* —as with *momlike, singalonglikes, sarongwise,* and *shapewise.* To spell such a neologism correctly, you once more have to determine which base word and suffixes would logically culminate in the overall meaning of the neologism. Usually, these neologisms are relatively easy to spell once you recognize the two parts, as with *lankly* and *bullyable.* Prefixes (a group of letters used at the beginning of a word) are also used to create neologisms, such as *unbusy* and *cybercar.* Prefixes and suffixes have long been used in popular culture to create new words, usually highly disposable neologisms. In the 1960s, the television show "Batman" seemed to mock this linguistic strategy by excessively "bat-izing" all manner of gadgets and devices—bat-mobile, batarang, bat-funnel, and the infamous shark repellent bat-spray, which surely pushed the bat-envelope for bat-prefixes.

I hope to have made a point about spelling in general: it is not just rote memorization or clicking the right button. With neologisms, for example, you must think logically and creatively about which words or phrases might have been carved up and reassembled to generate the meaning of the neologism. (For a real challenge, figure out the ancestry of these neologisms and what they might mean: *vidiot, junkstaposition,* and *parrotise.*)

Jargon: Slang on Steroids?

Even if you avoid informal neologisms such as those discussed so far, you might need to use technical, industrial, or medical neologisms. Such terms are referred to as *jargon*—highly specialized language of a given profession or specific group. However, jargonistic terms are not always neologisms. Jargon includes words that have been around for many years but are normally used only by specialists. For instance, *campanologist* has been used since at least 1857 to refer to a person highly skilled in ringing musical bells. But the term is rarely found outside the discourse of music scholars, bell manufacturers, and presumably campanologists.

Even hardcover dictionaries, especially the trimmer ones, might not indicate the spelling of jargon. Still, do not rule out using these "old-school" tools. A current, inclusive dictionary will usually include more words than a typical spell-checker does.

A recently produced spell-checker is usually unable to help spell jargon because these terms are relatively scarce (and perhaps too new). For most people, jargon poses greater spelling challenges than slang because the base words of jargon are often taken from Greek or Latin, as with *presbyopia* and *viremia.* Rather than learning these languages, you can best deal with jargon, as well as various types of neologisms, by prudently using one technological tool that is more reliable than spell-checkers: the Internet.

Being able to spell does not mean always being able to spell by yourself. Earlier, I lamented our increasing dependence on spell-checkers, but by no means am I discouraging their use, as long as we continue to improve our own understanding of spelling. To spell some words, every spelling bee champion has had to consult the Internet, a dictionary, a spell-checker, or even—shockingly enough—another human being. Often, in fact, that is what makes them good spellers: good spellers do not hesitate to consult an authoritative source.

You should not depend completely on technology, especially spell-checkers, but there is no shame in using the right tools to help you spell, especially with jargon, neologisms, homophones, and other "spelling demons" that confound even the most literate of people. Choose your tools wisely, and consider more than just spell-checkers. With such terms, the best place to start online is a respectable source, such as Merriam-Webster OnLine (m-w.com), the *McGraw-Hill Dictionary of Scientific and Technical Terms* (accessscience.com/Dictionary/dictionary .html), and Dictionary.com (dictionary.com). If you have access to a college library, you might be able to use other sources, including the *Oxford English Dictionary* Online. These sorts of Web pages allow you to check the meaning of the word as well as the spelling. Whereas spell-checkers are conducive to a mindless deferring to technology, checking your spelling by using online sources engages you in the decision, compelling you to think and learn as you determine which sources are trustworthy.

If these tools do not acknowledge the existence of a particular word that you think exists, you might then turn to a search engine such as Google. Beware of merely using Google or other search engines to type what you think is the correct spelling. The fact that you have dozens of hits does not mean you spelled the word correctly. Rest assured that any misspelling you can create has already appeared on the Web, and your "confirmations" might simply consist of people who misspelled the word the same way you did.

Nonetheless, if all else fails, look for neologisms and jargon on respectable websites. Check more than one, and consider the credibility of each site. "Country Bob's Blog of Things That Are *Really* Starting to Annoy Me" is probably not the best authority for how to spell *millefiori*, a term dealing with flowerlike designs. An art museum's website would likely be a superior resource.

With many search engines, including Google, you can type *definition* plus the word in question to obtain a list of sites that define the word. Google also attempts to spell-check your search requests, but this spell-checker is even more dubious than those provided with word processors. Don't trust it.

A related type of spelling challenge is the acronym — a word or abbreviation formed by using the initials of different words (such as *AWOL*, *TV*, or *FBI*). Some people insist that a true acronym must be pronounceable as a whole word (*WAC*), as opposed to sounding out each letter (*GDI*). Here, I use the term in a general sense to include any sort of word formed through using initials.

Acronyms are used to produce neologisms, slang, and jargon. Perhaps because they seem more like initials than true words, there seem to be few rules on how acronyms are created, discarded, or used, making it difficult to anticipate their spelling. Sometimes, an acronym undergoes a makeover; letters are added or rearranged to allow it to have new functions and meanings. *TWOC*, for example, stands for "take without owner's consent," but it has given rise to *twoccer* — a person who takes things, especially cars, without the owner's permission. Occasionally, an acronym becomes so acceptable that most people do not even realize that the term was once an abbreviation. The word *laser*, for instance, was once shorthand for "<u>l</u>ight <u>a</u>mplification by <u>s</u>timulated <u>e</u>mission of <u>r</u>adiation." A word such as *laser*, *radar*, or *scuba* is arguably no longer an acronym at all, having joined the sanctified world of words and not standing for anything other than itself.

Acronyms are used in many professions, especially engineering, computer industries, and the government. At times, the love of acronyms is so vast that acronyms are embedded within acronyms—like a Russian nesting doll that has another wooden doll tucked inside. *NCT* stands for "NARTE Certified Technician," with *NARTE* standing for "National Association of Radio and Telecommunications Engineers." Acronyms are useful because they are succinct, and probably also because—like slang and jargon in general—they create a sense of community and power, which might account in part for the military establishment's inclination to use acronyms. Normally, only insiders and specialists can decipher them, meaning that the spelling of acronyms is important despite their borderline status as being words at all.

Acronyms have become increasingly popular in e-mail, text messaging, online discussion groups, and other emerging modes of communication. Acronyms are the fastest-growing type of neologism and are bound to the modern age. In fact, the term *acronym* was first used in the 1940s, and while it has long been common to abbreviate words by using their initials, the practice of pronouncing the result as a whole word (rather than merely of individually pronouncing each letter) was extremely rare before World War I. Perhaps the growth of acronyms is directly related to the rise of the modern industrial and technological eras, which for decades have introduced a stream of new products that need names—and in a hurry. Acronyms are created in assembly-line fashion, fusing assorted parts to produce a functional if not attractive product that is all set for easy consumption.

In any case, you cannot memorize the thousands of acronyms used in professional settings and in casual discourse.

The following are just a few acronyms that reflect the diverse contexts in which they are used:

- **AAR:** air-to-air refueling
- **AIDS:** acquired immune deficiency syndrome
- **ATEG:** Assembly for the Teaching of English Grammar
- **BTW:** by the way
- **ERIC:** Education Resources Information Center
- **FAA:** Federal Aviation Administration
- **GIF:** graphic interchange format
- **IMO:** in my opinion
- **JPEG:** Joint Photographic Experts Group
- **LAB:** low-altitude bombing
- **NASCAR:** National Association for Stock Car Auto Racing
- **NATO:** North Atlantic Treaty Organization
- **NCD:** nanocrystalline diamond
- **PCT:** paranoid conspiracy theorist
- **SHIELD:** Strategic Hazard Intervention Espionage Logistics Directorate
- **TESOL:** teaching English to speakers of other languages
- **WOMBAT:** waste of money, brains, and time
- **WYSIWYG:** what you see is what you get (pronounced *wiz-ee-wig*)

If an acronym is pronounced by merely uttering each letter one at a time (as with *DDT*), the spelling is usually a nonissue unless you cannot remember the correct letters or you mishear the term.

Other acronyms are more problematic in terms of spelling. All acronyms confuse spell-checkers. Acronyms are so confusing that usually the spell-checker's default setting is to ignore every word composed solely of capital letters. When you use acronyms and need to check their spelling, hardcover and online dictionaries are usually no better than spell-checkers. As with jargon, the best resource may be an online search engine that allows you to check the spelling at credible websites.

Needless to say, avoid using any acronyms unless you are certain your readers know what they mean. Unless the acronym is commonplace for all your readers, spell out the words in their entirety the first time you use them, placing the acronym afterward in parentheses. That act can also help you confirm the spelling of the acronym, because *normally* an acronym is based on the first letters of each word.

Such is not the case with one type that pushes the limit of what we mean by *acronym*. These acronyms are particularly informal and are only loosely derived from the actual initials or spelling of their base words, as with *Humvee* standing in a contorted way for "high-mobility multipurpose wheeled vehicle." The conversational writing found on the Internet, especially in chat rooms and instant messaging, is replete with these acronyms. Consider, for example, *CUL8R* ("see you later"), *SUP* ("What's up?"), and *F2F* ("face to face"). These abbreviations are often based more on slipshod pronunciation of the base words than on their spelling.

Informal words, including slang and neologisms, are more useful than you might have been taught. In some situations, they are handy and thought provoking. Despite their spelling difficulties, it is worth the effort to determine the correct spelling when these words can be effectively used.

Still, I am not inclined to commend the proliferation of acronyms, even if I am saying we should spell them correctly when we must use them. Undoubtedly, they are efficient. In emergency situations, abbreviations can help save lives when time is of the essence. In the midst of battle, "Get in your Humvee!" is more expedient than "Get in your high-mobility multipurpose vehicle!" Chances are slim an English teacher would appear amid the smoke and debris to offer a more formal language option.

Abbreviations can also be eye-catching and cute—as with *gr8* rather than *great*. But too often people use acronyms just because they can. With some acronyms, it is dubious to claim they are saving time or space. How much longer does it take to type out *before* instead of *b4*? Is it really cute the twentieth time we see this abbreviation?

Internet chat and text messaging are conducive to acronyms that take the place of longer phrases. Some of the tiny keyboards compel us to abbreviate whenever possible to avoid the tediousness of pressing impossibly tiny letters, though I have to wonder if the best time-saving method would be to not send the silly text message in the first place. I can understand why acronyms are useful with supermodern, megaminiaturized technology that makes even the best typist resort to pecking away with a paper clip, but one growing trend is to create acronyms for hackneyed language. Consider such gems as *LAB&TYD* ("life's a bitch and then you die"), *PLMKO* ("Please let me know, OK?"), and *ROFLGO* ("rolling on floor laughing guts out"). Even the name sometimes given this variety of language is severely abbreviated: *txtspk* (textspeak). Determining the meaning and spelling of such abbreviations is not the true problem: people are simply not taking time to communicate meaningfully with one another.

Technology provides us unlimited opportunities to communicate, whether we have anything to say or not. Communication typically lacks depth when we are multitasking—communicating with faceless individuals while also word processing, answering e-mail, text messaging, or playing video

games. Hewlett-Packard commissioned a study on how workers were affected by such multitasking (not counting video
games). The study found an average decrease of ten points in
the IQ scores of workers who tried to keep up with the
onslaught of incoming messages. Fortunately, the effects were
temporary, and the workers were not truly any "dumber." They
simply could not focus on what they were doing. A ten-point
drop, though, is equivalent to losing an entire night's sleep and
must take its toll on a person's ability to communicate. Perhaps
the excess of acronyms in technological communication is a
reflection of the dumbing down of language as a means of cop-
ing with diminished thought. Or perhaps banal abbreviations
naturally occur when we are engaged in banal conversations.

So much for quality time.

An excess of abbreviations emerges when our purpose is
merely to send or respond to a message, rather than communicate something meaningful. At this rate, we will soon see
abbreviations that take the place of entire paragraphs and
documents. Technology allows us to do things quickly, but
maybe we should slow down, taking time to communicate
meaningfully.

If poorly spelled words and cryptic acronyms were limited
to electronic chatter, it might not be a significant problem, just
another Internet eyesore. These language choices, however, can
become a habit, carrying over to more significant discourse.
Some people assert that everyone surely understands when we
should write in webspeak and when we should follow the conventions of formal writing. Their assertions, however, are no
more true than claiming everyone also knows when to use
informal speech and when not to. The truth is that any aspect
of casual language—including cute misspellings and clumsy
acronyms—can become a habit.

Take, for instance, the case of a thirteen-year-old girl in Scotland who submitted an entire essay in "txtspk." Her first sentences are as follow:

My smmr hols wr CWOT. B4, we usd 2go2 NY 2C my bro, his GF & thr 3 :- kds FTF. ILNY, it's a gr8 plc.

For those who prefer English, this would read:

My summer holidays were a complete waste of time. Before, we used to go to New York to see my brother, his girlfriend, and their three screaming kids face to face. I love New York; it's a great place.

As reported in the *Daily Telegraph*, the student said she used txtspk because it is "easier than standard English." Easier for whom, we might inquire? Certainly not the intended reader.

It is similar to the problem with many people who interview for a job and forget to leave street talk at the door. The *Wall Street Journal* once referred to the phrase "I was like" as a verbal virus—a meaningless but harmless phrase until it spreads to formal communication, such as job interviews. Just as trite phrases can spread to speech situations in which we want to be taken seriously, so can Internet misspellings and obscure abbreviations make their way into formal writing.

For readers curious about the three jargonistic terms I mentioned but did not define, here are their meanings:

- **vidiot:** someone who plays too many video games
- **junkstaposition:** two or more automobiles, usually of dubious quality, parked next together
- **parrotise:** a haven for exotic birds

Do Spelling Bees Pollinate?

pelling seems more lonely than being a Democrat in Texas. That might be true when you are all alone on Friday night looking up *camaraderie* in the dictionary, yet at its core spelling is a communal activity.

As with any set of conventions or rules indicating how we are supposed to use "proper" English, spelling is a social construction. Spelling per se is not found in nature but is instead a pragmatic tool devised by a community, or by the part of society that has the power to make spelling rules. In any language, spelling is ultimately a subjective matter, and spelling systems often reflect the speech preferences or habits of some members of the community more than others. We are not taught to think this way about spelling, grammar, or language. Usually, these are simply taught as The Rules, as though there were no other logical alternatives. This issue will be clearer later in this book as I discuss the peculiar history of English spelling, but my point for now is that spelling ultimately reflects an attempt to create a shared code among members of a diverse community. Thus, to understand what spelling is really about, we must again move beyond words, beyond any one individual's spelling demons.

We must view spelling as a social happening.

One social side of spelling involves the obvious fact that most writing has an audience. Not too long ago, many curmudgeons were foretelling the demise of writing and reading as arts that were increasingly lost on young people. The power and popularity of the written word was allegedly being undermined by telephone chatter, television sitcoms, and distracting hip movements associated with rock-and-roll music—all of which was leading to the final closing of a mythical golden age during which young and old alike had relied on the printed word for all their amusement and learning needs.

No doubt, the fall of Western civilization might be impending, but it's not because printed words are in short supply. The Internet alone has provided innovative opportunities for people to exhibit their writing skills, and these public displays can have a lengthy shelf life. Even today, I am able to observe a misspelling I committed more than ten years ago in a casual e-mail someone posted on an educational website. Spelling is a social act that will not go away.

Spelling Bees in America

We most clearly see the social side of spelling in the myriad spelling bees held each year in Nebraska farm towns as well as in the nation's capital. These competitions typically involve young students who publicly demonstrate their spelling prowess as they listen to words that they must then spell—usually in sudden-death style with one misspelling leading to automatic elimination. The spelling bee's surprising popularity offers a focal point for understanding why spelling is a larger, more important matter than one might have guessed.

The best-known spelling contest is the National Spelling Bee, sponsored since 1941 by media giant E. W. Scripps Company. The final stage of the national championship began many years earlier with nine contestants in 1925 and has grown to include some 250 students from not only the United States but sites around the globe, such as Guam, Mexico, Jamaica, American Samoa, Saudi Arabia, and Japan. Today, the organizers of the National Spelling Bee indicate its primary goal is "to help students improve their spelling, increase their vocabularies, learn concepts, and develop correct English usage that will help them all their lives." In the 1930s, the organizers candidly admitted that a primary goal was "increasing general interest among pupils in a dull subject."

In recent years, some nine million students have participated each year in the sequence of contests that progress from classrooms to regional levels, culminating in Bee Week and the Super Bowl of bees—the National Spelling Bee. The first round of the national competition is a written test, but thereafter kids are onstage, under the lights and cameras, with dozens of parents, spelling coaches, and reporters seated in the audience.

During two intense days, these kids go through polysyllabic words as if they were Happy Meals. Preparing the word list is a closely guarded process that begins almost a year before the contest. Each word on the list is carefully ranked according to the alleged difficulty of its spelling, but the process is not a science. Depending on a person's background, words in later rounds might be relatively common or infuriatingly obscure. The final words to be given out have included *croissant* and *abalone* (which might be particularly familiar to contestants who visit fine restaurants) as well as *odontalgia* and *pococurante* (which might be familiar only to people who make word lists for spelling bees).

The national contest is not very forgiving. Each year, a few slips of the tongue result in elimination for several children, who try so hard to stop the wrong letter from escaping their lips that they leave skid marks in their mouths. But to no avail.

Contestants are not allowed to change an answer. Once even a single letter is uttered, it cannot be taken back. This might seem harsh until you remember that parents are among the spectators. It's not hard to imagine how parents' body language could—unintentionally, of course—indicate to their child that they believe a misspelling is in progress (never mind that the child, not the parent, is usually the household spelling expert).

The name itself—*spelling bee*—suggests the social nature of the competitions. Although the lexical origins of *spelling bee* are not known for a fact, one older use of *bee* refers to a gathering of people who engage in an activity (such as barn raising or quilting) in order to help a member of their community. This use of *bee* is usually considered American in origin, and spelling bees are likewise considered an American institution, even though contests similar to spelling bees have been held in other countries. French-based schools in Quebec, for instance, hold an annual spelling bee—*Concours D'allation*. Most overseas bees, such as those held in Britain, are not nearly as competitive or widely known as their American counterparts.

The insect bee is a fascinating creature—busy, social, always ready to lend a hand, leg, or mandible to any of its fifty thousand neighbors. Bees do not help just members of their hive. They help numerous species—from wildflowers to people—through pollination. Bees wantonly fly from plant to plant keeping vegetation alive—along with the hive, other insects, humans, and any higher life forms that ultimately depend on plant life.

I like to think spelling bees also pollinate, at least in a cultural sense. Spelling bees, too, go from place to place keeping ideas alive—ideas that benefit the human hive. These bees constitute one way in which people are reminded that one person's spelling affects not just the individual but the larger group as well, if for no other reason than the fact that misspellings hamper communication. Every spring, hundreds of newspapers, television stations, and websites proudly note how a local student is representing the community (or sometimes a whole country) at a spelling bee. Even in times when it has been fashionable to brand spelling as trivial, spelling bees are there to remind a new generation, classroom by classroom, that correct spellings really do exist and are valued.

If spelling were as lonesome an act as it might seem on the surface, people would not give bees much attention. If anything, however, Americans are increasingly drawn to spelling bees. A growing number of senior citizens, and not just those trying to relive the glory days of their youth, are holding their own bees to help them be mentally and socially active. Winners of the National Spelling Bee once had to be content with an invitation to meet with the president of the United States. Nowadays, they are in great demand on the talk-show circuit and might actually meet Oprah. Spelling bees have been the subject of novels, an award-winning film documentary (*Spellbound*), at least two feature movies, and even a Broadway musical (*The 25th Annual Putnam County Spelling Bee*). The phenomenon is not exactly new, however. Transmitted live from BBC studios in 1938, "Spelling Bee" is now considered TV's first quiz show. It consisted of a host, dressed as a schoolmaster, who would ask a panel of adult guests to spell words correctly. The show did not last long, but years later the concept returned. Since 1994, the final rounds of the National Spelling Bee have been televised live, not on public broadcasting networks but on ESPN.

Perhaps some misguided individuals tune in hoping that, this year, maybe spelling will finally be a contact sport, while others watch to see who loses rather than who wins. Some people go to auto races to see the crashes. Similarly, many viewers catch the national bee on ESPN just to watch brainy kids who, after cruising through early laps in the contest, are sideswiped by *autochthonous* or slam into impenetrable *wallydraigle*.

The appeal of the bee, though, goes beyond sadistic rubber-necking. But before considering other reasons why the contests receive considerable attention and respect, we should first note the murmurings of certain members of the hive who do not believe spelling bees are propagating anything of value.

Taking a Stand Against Literacy?

In 2004, school officials for the Lincoln School District in Rhode Island unanimously voted to abolish spelling bees in grades four to eight. They felt the bees did not meet the goals of the federal No Child Left Behind Act because the contests did not help *all* students reach high standards and because of concerns over the feelings of students who did not win. Assistant Superintendent Linda Newman said, "It's about one kid winning, several making it to the top, and leaving all others behind. That's contrary to No Child Left Behind." The official went on to explain that spelling bees do not build self-esteem in all students, nor do the contests allow students to "believe they're all winners."

When educators say such things, it almost makes me want to be against self-esteem. What they forget is that true self-esteem occurs when people are given a difficult task and succeed, or when they do not succeed yet realize they will better themselves if they keep trying.

In 2005, Lincoln school officials reversed their decision and reinstated the bees, after numerous complaints from parents, teachers, and community leaders. So far, the district has not found a need to provide trauma counseling to the hundreds of students who did not win a spelling contest.

Other detractors can be seen at the national championship in Washington, DC. In recent years, a half dozen protesters have picketed the site of the finals. No, this isn't a group of good ol' boys chugging down a few brewskies and waving signs reading, "Down with Litracy!" This is a group of well-intended (but terribly confused) members of the American Literacy Society and the Simplified Spelling Society. These fervent men and women bear signs that read, "I'm thru with through," "Spelling Shuud Bee Lojical," and "Spell different differnt" (signs that, to me, are essentially saying, "Down with Literacy!").

The protestors complain that bees reinforce the arbitrary spellings that lead to dyslexia, illiteracy, and harder lives for immigrants trying to learn English. Sanford Silverman, one picketer and an advocate of developing new rules for spelling, believes the illogical system of English spelling has kept many people functionally illiterate. He explains, "If these people were able to read and write with a simplified spelling system, they would be able to fill out a job application, stay employed, and stay out of prison."

English spelling is, as we all know, frequently illogical, and the rules for how to use any language will indeed by nature penalize some individuals more than others. These demonstrators are not completely wrong in their ideals and logic, just in their timing and own spelling. As a result of their public lamentations, the protestors are given an opportunity to appear in the media, and everyone has the right to appear foolish and be seen on CNN. But they are certainly not furthering their cause by waving baffling signs at the national bee. While they offer amusement to bee contestants and spectators, they do little more than make people appreciate the sensibility of knowing how to spell English as we know it, especially when the alternative is spelling words as they appear on the protestors' signs.

More than Memorizing

I have heard other people deride spelling bees by saying they are a big to-do about nerdy kids who are able to memorize

thousands of obscure words. That is like claiming the NBA
championship is about how many times a few lanky million-
aires can put an orange ball through an eighteen-inch hoop.
Succeeding in any one endeavor means being capable with
many skills, and these skills are often just as significant, if not
more so, than the primary activity itself. In spelling as well as
basketball championships, winners exhibit qualities that are
not only useful for the individual but also admired—and perhaps greatly needed—by society.

Spelling bee contestants and champions frequently go on to
become valued members of their communities. For example,
the very first national champion, Frank Neuhauser, received a
hero's welcome upon his return to Louisville in 1925 and later
became a successful patent attorney. Such individuals do not
become successful because of their spelling, but undoubtedly
the skills and qualities they hone for spelling bees can help
them in many ways.

As a later chapter will discuss in more detail, memorization
is a huge factor in spelling, but so is the ability to solve problems and think rationally. Even the best speller will eventually
have to make an educated, logical guess—a guess based on an
understanding of language features such as prefixes, suffixes,
word origins, meaning, and grammatical function. Spelling
podiatrist is easier if you realize it refers to a "foot doctor" and
recall that *pod-* is a morpheme meaning *foot* and has nothing to
do with an iPod. It is even easier if you recall the fairly common use of *-iatrist* to mean *doctor* (as in *psychiatrist*). But the
aspiring champion cannot be seduced into assuming that a
word will always be rationally spelled based on such features,
for some words are spelled in an illogical or peculiar way. For
instance, the only word in English to have two *i*'s in a row is
skiing, while *angry* and *hungry* are the only two that end in *-gry*.
Spelling is the most difficult type of logic puzzle: one based
only partially on logic.

Spelling bees are a symbol of how our culture appreciates literacy, but they are also about hard work and perseverance. Perhaps that explains why America in particular is fond of spelling bees. The contests reflect a key democratic ideal: if a person just works hard enough, he or she can succeed even in the most competitive situations. For contestants and spectators alike, spelling bees demonstrate that young people must prepare themselves before entering the competitive arenas of adulthood, whether these arenas be spelling contests, commerce, or the pursuit of a suitable spouse. It is no accident that spelling bees have focused on sending this reminder to impressionable children, preparing them to become hardworking contributors to their community and nation.

Indeed, a staggering amount of time and energy is needed to get ready for the National Spelling Bee. Contestants read voraciously (another skill just as important as spelling itself), but they train in other ways as well. Many read and reread dictionaries, wearing out the pages as they consult these books. In addition, studying for a bee does not mean studying by oneself. Most contestants work with their parents and other students, often through the Internet or even text messaging on cell phones. Some hire tutors or receive help from volunteers, but all contestants train hard to learn and to win.

All contestants are expected to know approximately 3,800 difficult-to-spell words listed in a study aid entitled *Paideia*. Many contestants not only write down these words in a notebook but also make notes on the pronunciation, meaning, and origin of each word. And much more is needed to advance in the final rounds. The 2005 champ was thirteen-year-old Anurag Kashyap. Jim Dyer, his English teacher and coach, commented on the effort Kashyap put into the contest: "We've been studying together once a week for two years. He's an amazing kid who's studied more than one hundred thousand words."

It is easy to forget that spelling is about words, not just letters. Spelling and vocabulary are highly interrelated — complementary and truly inseparable, except within the skewed classrooms of teachers who fixate solely on either phonics or whole-language techniques. Separating the spelling of a written word from its meaning is like trying to separate Saturn from its rings. It requires too much effort and only diminishes what we study. When Kashyap and other spellers learn one hundred thousand words, they do not merely learn how to place letters in a particular order. They study meanings of the words, and words are the starting point for ideas.

Researchers have found that highly successful businesspeople, just to name one sphere of society, tend to have much larger-than-average vocabularies than most individuals. One reason these businesspeople might be so successful is that they are familiar with more ideas and are able to draw on the words that best describe a situation or problem. Finding the right word offers all of us a semantic foothold — a way to help us in the uphill struggle of clearly expressing a complex idea. Being able to spell means becoming familiar with more and more words, which in turn leads to being able to understand and express more and more ideas.

Spelling thus reflects several valuable skills that society respects, but I am not claiming that every successful person or great thinker must be able to spell particularly well. Albert Einstein and George Washington were poor spellers, and even authors such as F. Scott Fitzgerald and Agatha Christie struggled with spelling. Some evidence indicates a form of dyslexia or a neurological problem prevents many people from spelling effectively, even if they read voluminously or write well in other regards. The vast majority of people, however, can improve their spelling — while also improving a range of other skills. Perhaps that is one reason why most spelling bee contestants excel in subjects besides spelling. Kashyap, for example, participated in other academic contests, including Mathcounts, Science Olympiad, and the California Geographic Bee. If nothing else, the attention that spelling bees place on academic success can focus a student's attention on other subjects as well.

Literacy, wordsmithery, logic, hard work—these are all embedded within preparing for a spelling bee, yet even more skills and qualities are associated with bees. A good speller has to be exact; being "in the ballpark" is not good enough. Contestants also have to be able to concentrate under pressure, because they are not allowed to buy a vowel or phone a friend. Imagine standing in front of an audience (not to mention TV cameras) and being asked to spell *lederhosen*, especially if you are from Walnut Creek, California, and have never been to Bavaria, where people wear this type of leather shorts. In a contest involving hundreds of excellent spellers, winning often comes down to who can remain focused the longest in a high-pressure situation.

My point has been twofold. First, bees entail a wider range of skills than most people realize, and so does learning to spell in general. The remarkable children who win these contests learn a great deal in the process, but even we other mortals hone numerous skills when we improve our spelling.

Second, spelling is acutely social in nature, and bees highlight this social aspect. These contests are not nerdfests that are of interest only to the spelling obsessed. Bees help create and maintain social cohesion by propagating a few key values that help hold our communities together: namely, competition can be good, perseverance (besides being difficult to spell) has its rewards, and laurels are still given out for being notably literate. Spelling bees aside, being able to spell likewise has a far-reaching social dimension, for there are larger values entrenched within it. No wonder, then, that people have such strong reactions to misspellings and, rightly or not, make all kinds of inferences as a result.

The "hidden values" packed into spelling and spelling bees help explain why many recent contestants and winners have been children of immigrant families. Indian-Americans in particular are well represented in today's spelling bees. Although making up less than 1 percent of the American population, they have in recent years accounted for 10 to 15 percent of the participants at the national competition. In 2005, the top-four finishers were of Indian ancestry, with Anurag Kashyap taking first place. The keen interest among the Indian-American community began in 1985 when thirteen-year-old Balu Natarajan (now a doctor of sports medicine) won the national bee. Unlike a great many immigrants, Indian-Americans often arrive in America being able to speak and write English fluently, and these families are still influenced by an Indian educational system emphasizing recitation and memorization. Yet, as with most immigrants, Indian-Americans are not always given the same opportunities as other Americans, nor given full respect as being Americans and fitting into the national culture. Natarajan proved to his community that here was an aspect of the American educational system in which they could excel. Indeed, a few years after Natarajan's victory, Indian-American organizations set up a series of contests to prepare Indian-Americans for regional and national spelling competitions.

While spelling English might be humdrum to some members of mainstream America, it is a formidable accomplishment and a precious symbol for families who migrate to pursue what they view as the American dream of democracy, freedom, and upward mobility. Literacy, the right to compete fairly, and academic achievement—these are taken for granted by most Americans, but not by immigrants with vivid memories of places where such ideals do not flourish, at least not as they supposedly do in the United States.

In defending the contests, Paige Kimble, director of the Scripps National Spelling Bee and 1981 champion, once said that bees are "like apple pie in America." They indeed are an important slice of Americana, so it is no wonder why many immigrants see that winning a bee helps the larger ethnic community as well as the individual student. Winning a bee is a symbol of how the student and his or her larger community can compete with any American and, more important, how they all have the potential to make a positive contribution to American society.

Even if you still think of spelling as a solitary performance, I think you will agree that a misspelling can be a very public demonstration. Spelling bees constitute one of the few times when people come together to praise correct spelling. When is the last time you read a sentence and said, "Boy, that was some great spelling that writer did!" Ordinarily, we pay heed to a person's spelling ability only when he or she errs, so think well of spelling bees if for no other reason than their attempt to provide a little balance in the way we react to the arrangement of letters.

Ancient Warriors and Modern Spelling

I think I hav been patient long enuf. . . . I have a much better use for twenty-five thousand dollars a year.

—ANDREW CARNEGIE (1915), giving up a twelve-year campaign to simplify English spelling

ultimillionaire Andrew Carnegie is one of many people who have argued in favor of overhauling English in hopes that our spelling system could be more consistent, more logical, and easier to learn. Nobody has ever succeeded in fully meeting this goal. An occasional victory is achieved when one errant word or another is brought into greater conformity with the spelling of similar words. Yet such piecemeal changes often mean there is more than one way to spell the word in question, thereby increasing the unpredictability of English spelling rather than decreasing it.

No matter how much money is thrown at the problem, the Spelling Revolution will not occur in our lifetime nor in that of our children's children. We might as well initiate a fund drive to change the way the sun rises. Our imperfect system of spelling is so entrenched within our history, culture, and economy that it will not be seriously altered except through the normal channels of slow linguistic change—the ongoing, unpredictable development of language, which is just as likely to lead to greater complexity as to greater simplicity.

In Chapter 7, I will discuss spelling reforms in more detail, but for now, consider just a few obstacles to an expeditious "top-down" approach to language change—one that would have us officially adopt a spelling system created by supposed experts:

- Millions of adults, not to mention children, would need to start over again in learning to spell. Try telling that to an eighty-year-old English teacher.
- For children who learn the new system as their only form of written English, millions of existing books, magazines, newspapers, and Web pages would be almost unreadable if a major change in spelling were made, making these texts practically useless to future generations.
- Chances are that the new system, to be truly better, would need to revise our existing alphabet, taking out some letters and adding others. Imagine what that would mean economically in terms of replacing computer keyboards and telephone keypads.
- If we really want the change to be effective, all English-speaking countries would have to agree on the new system, as if even one country could come to agreement.
- Who will enforce the changes, and how? It would take stern federal laws directed not only at schools but at the business and manufacturing world. Chances are that private enterprise would not support such a move unless it resulted in increased revenue. If the lords of commerce oppose the new system, rest assured our legislators will balk as well.

Some people reasonably argue for an entirely new script rather than working with our flawed alphabet. Would we use the Visible Speech alphabet created by Alexander Melville Bell, whose son invented the telephone? In this system, each symbol resembles the anatomical position it creates within the vocal tract—an ingenious scheme developed for hearing-impaired people. Personally, I would opt for a less rational but more romantic option: Tengwar, the script invented by J. R. R. Tolkien to represent the languages of his Middle-Earth. Perhaps we could use this as an opportunity to reinvent our cultural identity, just as the pop singer Prince once reinvented himself by using a cryptic symbol in place of his name.

Most Americans have become attached to the present spelling system, irregularities and all. In theory, everyone would agree we need to do something about the system, just as we agree in principle that tax reforms are needed. The rub is always in the details, for it is the details that affect us individually.

Think about proper nouns alone. In contrast to a common noun, a proper noun is the particular name of a person, place, or thing. The term *proper* is derived from the Latin word *proprius*, which deals with ownership; the same root word is used to form *property*. We think of our names not just as our property but as an orthographic extension of ourselves—as a symbol of our identity and existence. Despite the old rhyme about sticks and stones breaking bones, calling people by a name that they do not accept is definitely not the act of a peace-loving man or woman.

A recent study, "How Do I Love Thee? Let Me Count the Js," (*Journal of Personality and Social Psychology*, 2004) indicates names can also be a source of harmony between individuals. By examining marriage records and surveying college students, the researchers found that men and women are more likely to be attracted to one another and even marry when their names are similar, such as having the same initials. The effect seems especially strong when people are under stress or feel insecure. Our names are so central to defining who we are that we seem to find comfort in a potential mate having a name sharing similar sounds or letters. (This might explain why Superman, whose real name was Kal-El, had a difficult time choosing between Lois Lane and Lana Lang.) Looking at someone's initials seems an odd way to choose a spouse, but obviously name identification is just one factor. People also take into account more sensible factors, such as eye color and other meaningful physical attributes.

My last name should logically be spelled *Beesun*, but you would have to tear the *a* and *o* of my name from my cold, dead keyboard. Easily done perhaps, but try telling the front line of the Oakland Raiders that their names will be changed as determined by the Committee on Un-Amerikan Spellings. Although few of us have any personal investment in the spelling of *fish* or *enough*, we are attached to our own names and the names of places special to us, yet these would be fair game in a brave new world of reformed English spelling.

Aside from a fling here and there with the spelling of a few words, we are married to existing ways of spelling—more than married because there is no chance of divorce. We would have a happier union if we realize that English indeed has a difficult spelling system but is not as ghastly as portrayed by well-intended individuals who would woo us with fantasies of an ideal alternative. Nor is the system truly chaotic. Our spellings are a direct result of a rich history involving contributions of diverse peoples.

To understand both the complexity and consistency of our present system, we must understand its convoluted past. The history of English is particularly complex and frequently peculiar, and these qualities show up in today's spellings. Looking at spelling from a historical perspective will also make it clear that there is at least one more major reason why a substantial revision of our current system is, beyond any shadow of a doubt, pointless.

The Dawn of English

As with most modern languages, English spelling more or less reflects an attempt to put spoken words onto paper. Thus, several features of speech affect spelling, not just pronunciation but also vocabulary and grammar. The history of spelling does not begin with written English but with the origins of spoken English.

Many aspects of English spelling can be traced to the earliest days of English — back to what is now called "Old English." In fact, much of today's everyday English vocabulary is derived from Old English, especially words that deal with the basics of life or with acts and things particularly important to primitive rural peoples (such as *stone, ship, mother, helmet, goose,* and *love*). The spelling of such words often does not reflect today's pronunciation because these ancient words have been through so much — hundreds of years of changing speech patterns and meanings.

Old English is older than most people realize, much older than the English spoken by either Geoffrey Chaucer or Frank Sinatra. This stage of English extends from roughly 500 A.D. to 1100 A.D. Even though Old English is the first form of what we consider English, the average English speaker of today would not recognize even the general topic of this Old English text:

> Gesæt ða on næsse niðheard cyning,
> þenden hælo abead heorðgeneatum,
> goldwine Geata. Him wæs geomor sefa,
> wæfre ond wælfus, wyrd ungemete neah,

se ðone gomelan gretan sceolde,
secean sawle hord, sundur gedælan
lif wið lice, no þon lange wæs
feorh æþelinges flæsce bewunden.

Old and Modern English differ not only in terms of spelling
but in sentence structure and the functions of words as well.
Even format differs; as seen in the above passage, a space
within a line of poetry would reflect the pause associated with
the rhythms of spoken Old English. Thus, translating texts
such as *Beowulf* is more complex than just converting a given
word into a modern equivalent. Here is one translation of the
passage, courtesy of Professor John Halbrooks:

The courageous king sat on the bluff;
Wished good luck to his hearth-companions,
Gold-friend of the Geats. His mind was mournful,
Restless and ready for death, fate was very near,
It shall come to the old man in the end,
Seek the treasure of his soul, break apart
The soul and body; it was not for much longer
That the life of the king would be grasped in flesh.

This passage from *Beowulf*, an Anglo-Saxon account of a leg-
endary Scandinavian hero, might seem more akin to Klingon
than to today's English; it indicates how a few words such as
on apparently have more preservative power than a Twinkie.
Such words have maintained their spelling for a thousand years
or more. However, most of today's words that can be traced
back to Old English are mere echoes of their former selves. In
the *Beowulf* passage, *cyning* evolved into today's *king*, *wæs*
became *was*, and *flæsce* morphed into *flesh*. Changes in speech
patterns often account for these transformations, but as I will
soon discuss, other factors also came into play.

The *Beowulf* passage was written in 1000 A.D., toward the end of the Old English period. To understand today's English, we need to go back further, back to the fifth century, when a struggling Roman Empire had its fill of troublesome Britain and left the land to its original owners or to any invaders who wanted to try their hand at ruling these lands.

Typically, the history of Old English is the story of who influenced it, but it is also a tale of those who did *not* do so — in particular, the Celts (pronounced with a <k>). The impact of the Celts on English and spelling is surprisingly small, even though they were in a position to be major players. Having populated Britain for eons (perhaps from as long ago as 800 B.C.), the Celts brought the Iron Age to the British Islands, covered most of the region, and left behind potent genes that still permeate much of the English population. During this Cretaceous period of civilization in Britain, Celtic dialects were the T. rex and triceratops of the linguistic landscape, yet Modern English holds only a few Celtic fossils—a handful of geographical names such as *Dover* and *Thames*, along with the name of a once-great basketball team.

If the Celtic influence had lived up to its potential, our language and alphabet would be far different, yet who can say whether it would be simpler or more complex? One thing is almost certain. Had it not been for swarms of Germanic tribes who eventually moved into Celtic Britain, I would be not be referring to Old English, or writing in English for that matter. If we were alive at all, you might be reading in Celtic fashion: starting at the bottom of the page rather than the top. I would likely be writing in Celtic about the difficulties of spelling using *ogham*—a Celtic alphabet in which each letter resembles one of twenty trees deemed sacred by Druids of the British Isles. (Contrary to what New Age jewelers would now have us believe, Germanic tribes, not the Celts, used an alphabet composed of runes.)

But let's return to what did usher in Old English. The giant sucking sound you might have heard when Romans left Britain was followed by the clamor of warlike tribes arriving from the European continent. Well, that description is a bit overstated. The Romans did not shuffle away overnight, nor did the continental tribes arrive all at once to wave farewell to Roman legions. Once the empire withdrew, however, the control of Britain was up for grabs, and the peoples who populated Britain lost their opportunity for control to Europeans having more military power.

Starting about 450 A.D., Germanic intruders began arriving into what is now England, and the impact of their warrior culture would be felt for centuries as they slowly but inevitably took command. Strangely enough, English spelling of today is a result of the aggressive nature of ancient Germanic tribes, for they directly and indirectly caused a succession of invasions that brought a rich mixing of diverse languages and dialects to the foundling nation of England.

The invading tribes included the Angles, from whom we have the word *England*, along with the Saxons and Jutes. The invaders soon met their very distant relatives, the Celts. The term *invaders* might be unfair, for German tribes apparently were recruited by Celtic rulers to fight the Picts, another early inhabitant of Britain. Besides, the Celts were a loosely defined group of diverse tribes who never truly unified as a single national force in the British Isles or anywhere else for that matter, so although they occupied Britain after having been driven out of most of Europe, the Celts themselves were just one of many factions who for many hundreds of years had invaded the isles or arrived there as refugees.

The reunion between Celts and their continental kin was not a happy one, at least not for the Celts, who, despite having a home-court advantage, were routinely assimilated into the Anglo-Saxon population or forced into Scotland, Wales, and Ireland—not to say these are dreadful places to live, but nobody likes to be coerced into a change of address. Apparently, the once-formidable fighting skills of the Celts deteriorated while they were under the thumb of the Roman Empire. Another factor involves a plague, originating in the Mediterranean, that decimated British Celts in the sixth century. During an era when Anglo-Saxons were establishing their authority over both land and language, the Celts were, for whatever reason, walking toward the sidelines of history—a sad demise for a people who sprung three thousand years ago from central Europe to cover the continent along with parts of western Asia.

Despite Roman rule of England from about 44 A.D. to 410 A.D., Latin likewise had little direct influence on the early formation of spoken English, unlike the influence it had on early French and Spanish—accounting for why English grammar today in some regards has more in common with German than with French or Spanish. Latin did contribute many words to Old English that in modified form are still used today, especially religious and governmental terms such as *bishop* and *regal*. In fact, Latin words would for centuries seep into Middle and Modern English. However, Latin was not a major factor early on; estimates are that only a little more than a hundred Latin terms were used with any frequency from 450 A.D. to 650 A.D. We should not expect Latin to be particularly influential in the vernacular even when Rome ruled Britain. Romans were the landlords, yet they accounted for a fraction of the discourse uttered in Romano Britain.

Thus, early Old English was not greatly influenced by two noteworthy cultures (Romans and Celts) that controlled Britain up to the influx of the Anglo-Saxon tribes. This phenomenon had an effect on our present spelling system. Although Old English obviously had a foundation (the languages of the initial Germanic invaders), it lacked the relative stability and consistency of the established Latin and Celtic languages. The complexity of today's English is partially due to the way Old English made its way in the world.

Politics also encouraged irregularity in early Old English. Linguistic standardization is usually a result of a national desire, or dictate, for the populace to adopt the speech patterns found in the most prestigious part of the nation. Throughout much of the Old English period, however, there was no "British nation," only independent kingdoms (usually seven, depending on alliances). These kingdoms spoke the same language but in different dialects. Because no single kingdom dominated Britain until the middle of the ninth century, when Wessex emerged as the seat of power, no single dialect stood out as the standard. As a result, the word *and* might have been spelled and pronounced as *and* in some regions but as *ond* elsewhere.

Nonetheless, by 650 A.D. the assorted Anglo-Saxon invaders were no longer intruders at all. A couple of centuries after their arrival, they had "suddenly" become home owners and, if not quite ready to sip tea in private clubs, were the major cultural force of England. The Germanic trespassers had become Anglo-Saxon kingdoms, and their common tongue—despite the existence of distinct dialects—could no longer be considered a mere variant of a continental language.

Old English had clearly arrived. The geographic remoteness of Britain from the rest of Europe was a major factor in this development. The Anglo-Saxons' separation, albeit by a slender English channel, from their continental relations led to a distinct society as well as language. This would not be the last time geography would affect English and thus our present-day spelling.

The Ruin and Replacement of Runes

During the early Old English period, we also see one of the most important historical developments ever not only for spelling but for the whole of written English: the decline of runes, an alphabet favored by the invading Germanic tribes. There were different types of runic alphabets, but their over-all similarity to Greek and Latin alphabets indicates all runic alphabets shared a common ancestry with the Roman alphabet that is also the basis of our present alphabet. Despite this common lineage, the runes and English alphabet of today have notable differences.

Runes date back to at least the first century B.C. and were associated with Germanic tribes who spread to various parts of Europe. Often found on stone carvings, the runic script is exceptionally angular, without curves and circles that would be difficult to chisel or scrape onto hard surfaces. In fact, the modern word *writing* is derived from an old Germanic word meaning *scrape* or *rasp*, which is essentially how the Runic symbols had to be "written" onto wood, stone, bone, or even metal. (Not surprisingly, then, Old German did not contribute *erase* to our vocabulary, because it was difficult to erase a rune. Our word *erase* derives from the Latin term *eradere*, which means *scratch out* and also accounts for the word *rodent*. Roman authors did not use rats to erase words, even though today a computer mouse is instrumental in the process of deleting words and erasing files.)

The Viking invaders brought the runic alphabet to England, but seventh-century Christian missionaries, detecting the pagan themes implicit within runes, strongly discouraged their use. At first, this reaction seems strikingly similar to how certain evangelical Christians of today can find satanic messages lurking within lyrics of rock music or children's television shows. Nevertheless, the runes indeed have a long history of containing "hidden" messages.

In addition to serving as part of the runic alphabet, each rune had a special meaning, often derived from mythology (such as Norse giants and gods) or forces of nature (such as the wind). In fact, some "rune-using" people believed runes were a gift from the chief of the Norse gods, Odin. To gain knowledge, Odin speared himself to a tree and learned the secrets of the runes so he could pass along this knowledge to his worshippers. Although the runic alphabet practically disappeared as a major communication tool by the twelfth century, runes for centuries continued to be used as decoration and mystical symbols, including certain military insignias created by leading Nazis who had interests in the occult and Norse mythology.

The Christianization of England, as well as other European lands, led to the steady decline of the runic alphabet and the establishment of the Roman alphabet that is the basis of spelling today. However, the alphabet that emerged in Old English was not quite the same as the one we have now. In most regions, it did not include *j, u,* or *w,* and there were at least four symbols commonly used then that we no longer use today. (As I will discuss later, one of these four was a rune that was in for the long haul and slow to depart. Aptly named *thorn,* this rune would contribute to a spelling problem that persists to this day.)

Of particular importance is the fact that the runes were replaced by an alphabet that was also phonetic in nature. That is, both alphabets attempt to capture the sounds of speech, with each letter or vowel representing a particular sound. A phonetic alphabet is just one approach to putting speech onto paper. Contrast it to what is called a true morphographic system; this is what you find with most Chinese languages, where each symbol stands for a particular idea, not a sound.

If the runes had been maintained, or if an alphabet other than the Roman version had replaced it, Britain would have had a difficult time communicating in writing with other European nations—not only during the Old English period but thereafter.

As far as spelling is concerned, the Roman alphabet that emerged had inherent limitations that we still see. First, Modern English is based on at least forty sounds, depending on one's dialect and hearing ability. In contrast, our alphabet has only twenty-six letters, and even in Old English the match between the English and Roman alphabet was imperfect. For instance, Old English contained sounds not represented in this alphabet. Even though the alphabet evolved in an attempt to reflect spoken English, the system is still flawed. Three letters (*c*, *q*, *x*) duplicate sounds already represented by other letters or by combinations of letters, and most letters can stand for more than one sound. Second, English is often no longer phonetic in spelling because pronunciations have significantly changed over the centuries, while spellings have not kept up or not changed at all. The spelling of *knight*, for example, reflects the way it was spoken centuries ago when there were almost no "silent letters" that plague today's spellers.

The gradual replacement of runes with a Roman alphabet would forever affect our language and spelling. This substitution occurred slowly and during an era when the foundations of English were being altered by numerous competing forces. Given the tumultuous nature of the Old English period, it is a wonder that our language is as regular and simple as it is. Indeed, yet another group of visitors to England would leave their mark on Old English and Western civilization.

The Vikings: More Relatives Who Wouldn't Leave

Tribes from northern Germany accounted for not only Angles, Saxons, and Jutes; these tribes also included seafaring people who migrated to Scandinavian countries such as Denmark and Norway—home of the Vikings. The Angles had just put their name on the doorway of England when Norse relations arrived, and arrived, and stayed.

Viking invasions began in earnest in 793 and lasted until the next, and arguably last, set of invaders came to England in 1066. What began as plundering ended with substantial parts of Britain being conquered by Vikings. The invasions had a huge effect on Old English, and at times this would be a linguistic contribution fueled by fierce bloodshed.

At one point, the seemingly invincible Vikings came close to doing to Anglo-Saxon culture what the Anglo-Saxons did to Celtic society. Eventually, quite the opposite happened. The Vikings inadvertently promoted the development of a unified Anglo-Saxon country and hastened the move toward standardization and simplification of English. The reason for this turnabout was largely due to one man, King Alfred.

This king of Wessex, known today as Alfred the Great, persuaded other English kingdoms to fight with him against the Danish Vikings, who by 878 controlled roughly half of Britain. Alfred was so successful that the Norse conquest of Britain was brought to a standstill, an event that in itself is relevant to spelling because our language today would likely be Scandinavian had it not been for Alfred's victory.

Alfred was not content to chase and thwart Vikings; he wanted to unify the portion of England not under Norse control. As a result of Alfred's leadership, the Wessex kingdom became increasingly influential, helping its dialect gain the lead as the language choice of literate people throughout the Anglo-Saxon territory.

His contributions to the language did not stop there. Alfred fully realized a common language is a key factor in consolidating kingdoms and peoples, so he was active in promoting English as a major cultural and literary language. He rebuilt the school system and made sure English, rather than Latin, was the basis of education. The king himself learned Latin so he could lend a hand in translating Latin documents and literature into the English of his kingdom. Although King Alfred's linguistic policies are probably the most successful ever in terms of an organized reform of English, his version of Old English did not progress down a simple path toward the Wessex dialect.

Even with Alfred's linguistic and political victories, the Anglo-Saxon language was greatly affected by the Scandinavian invaders. The Vikings spoke Old Norse, which was close enough to the Germanic origins of Anglo-Saxon to enable Vikings and the English populace to communicate in a basic way—and not just to hurl insults at one another before battle. Despite Viking colonization of northern Britain, the Norse and Anglo-Saxons intermingled and cooperated. In fact, the most famous literature of Old English is the epic poem *Beowulf*, which is Scandinavian in its characters and settings.

This bonding resulted in profound changes in Old English. However, it is surprising that the Norse and Anglo-Saxons had any kind of group hug considering the ongoing invasions, the viciousness of their bloody battles, and the accompanying slaughter that culminated in the attempted genocide known as the St. Brice's Day Massacre of 1002. In that year, King Ethelred of England authorized what he deemed the best way to secure his power and end Viking invasions: the execution of all Danish people in England. The edict was not successful, but there were many atrocities, such as in Oxford where a church was burnt in order to kill the Danish people inside who had sought sanctuary. In retaliation for such massacres, King Sweyn of Denmark escalated the invasions to the extent that in 1013 he was declared King of England, with his son Canute succeeding him a year later. England was therefore united, but under Danish rule (until 1042 when Edward the Confessor acceded to the throne).

In the midst of their pillages and occupations, the Vikings left behind important linguistic baggage. Even during periods of unrest and war, the Norse and Anglo-Saxons desired to communicate with one another, yet their languages were not completely the same. In such situations, people simplify their speech, much like English merchants and natives of the Pacific Islands would one day speak a modified form of English to conduct trade. Anglo-Saxon speech made communication difficult because it was heavily inflected; that is, special endings were added to a word depending on how it was used in a sentence. For example, today most English nouns have only two basic forms: the base form and the *-s* form (as with *car* and *cars*). Old English nouns had as many as *six* forms. English spelling today would be much more difficult if this additional layer of complexity—inflections—had survived intact. The desire for the Norse and Anglo-Saxons to communicate was not the only factor that led to the erosion of inflections, a development that also paved the way for Middle English. Nevertheless, the Vikings undoubtedly accelerated this simplification.

Another Norse impact on today's spelling is that many common words of today are Scandinavian, having been taken up by the Anglo-Saxon population. For the most part, these Old Norse words have changed in form over the years, but their spelling still reflects a Scandinavian upbringing. Norse is the basis of many Modern English words that begin with the <sk> sound, including *sky*, *skirt*, *skin*, *skill*, *scorch*, *scrape*, and *scrub*. The Vikings helped keep this type of word alive in English. Previously the Anglo-Saxons mysteriously started turning <sk> words into <sh> words; for example, *scrin* became *shrine*. Other modern words derived from Old Norse are as follow:

bring	oaf
father	same
folk	sorrow
house	summer
law	take
leg	want
man	wife
mine	window
mire	wrong
mother	warrior

Some of these old words have an interesting and charming meaning, despite being considered plain now. For example, our common word *window* comes from a phrase meaning *wind's eye*, which makes sense if you think of windows made before we put glass on them. It makes me want to leave the window open, even on a windless day.

One major contribution involving pronouns would take hundreds of years to be accepted throughout Britain, yet it symbolizes the way the Norse and Anglo-Saxon people—as well as their languages—could coexist. The Norse gave us the personal pronouns *they, them,* and *their*. These are the plural versions of the Anglo-Saxon pronouns *it, he,* and *she* which predate the Viking invasions. The singular pronouns differ greatly from their plural counterparts, yet both pronouns and people managed to function effectively despite obvious differences.

In many ways, the spelling of any language becomes more complicated when it borrows words or grammatical features from another language, but as a whole the Scandinavian influence—despite the image we have of marauding Vikings—had a calming effect on English, simplifying it in important regards and enriching it by adding more flexibility and vocabulary. It was not exactly the golden age of the English language, especially considering that the vast percentage of English people could neither read nor write. Still, Old English provided a relatively stable, consistent system of spelling—the lull before a storm of yet more warriors.

The Difficult Middle Years

The history of spelling does not end with Old English. In truth, the next stage would provide even more changes to spelling, not all for the good.

Just as the Norse and Anglo-Saxons were evolving into an English community, political unrest—due in large part to the upheaval caused by Viking intrusions in many lands—resulted in the last successful invasion onto English soil: the Norman conquest of 1066. This event ushered in the Middle English period, a transitional stage lasting roughly from 1100 to 1500.

By the end of the tenth century, the English language was enjoying an era of stability in terms of spelling. The era was far from being a linguistic paradise, as there was not a one-to-one correlation between letters and sound. That is, in fact, the Holy Grail of orthography: the ideal "one-letter, one-sound" system that relatively few languages have ever obtained (modern Finnish, Spanish, and Latvian are some that come close). Late Old English was stable in terms of spelling, yet it had a few glitches. For example, consider the letters *i* and *y*. At one time in Old English, *i* and *y* stood for two sounds that Anglo-Saxons considered distinct. By 1000 A.D., these pronunciation differences were relatively minor, but one concept we must remember when looking at the history of spelling is that letters are always reluctant to disappear even when they are no longer needed. Both *i* and *y*, for example, are still used today to represent the <i> sound found in *sit* or *gym*.

Nonetheless, Wessex conventions for spelling provided a norm after centuries of considerable inconsistency. The aforementioned Christianization of England was another important factor behind the stabilization of written English. When missionaries "spread the word," they depended on the written word of the Bible. They proved a formidable force in spreading literacy throughout England, and much of their success depended on creating a coherent, stable form of written communication.

Ironically, our English spelling system is a victim of its own success. Many of the problems we face today in learning to spell can be traced back to the successful standardization of spelling during the late Old English period. The problem is that spelling was becoming standardized at a time when speech patterns were still changing, with more significant changes forthcoming because of the Norman invasion.

Linguisticus Interruptus

Normally, real change in a language proceeds about as quickly as a supersized oil tanker moving through a shallow Louisiana swamp. Sometimes, though, a single event puts a halt to one course of development for a language and navigates it in another direction.

In 1066, the successful intrusion of William the Conqueror into Sussex interrupted the tumultuous but prolific intertwining of languages and dialects that had peaked with the relative stability of late Old English.

According to some scholars, almost all linguistic changes that resulted after the Norman Conquest of 1066 had already been under way for years, but there is no doubt that the success of the invasion kicked the evolutionary mechanisms of language into high gear, greatly accelerating the evolution of English and moving it in new directions. The conquest marks one of the great turning points of Western civilization. Legend has it that King Harold died after being shot in the eye with an arrow, but there is no debate that the defeat of his English troops at the Battle of Hastings profoundly changed the world—in so many ways, in fact, that we might overlook the impact on spelling.

The invasion was another in the line of Norse invasions that had gone on for centuries. Normandy is located in France, yet large portions of this region were settled in the ninth century by Norse Vikings (the name *Normandy* is adapted from *Norsemen* or *Northmen*). This settlement occurred in much the same way that the Norse had conquered much of Britain. This distant Norse relationship indirectly prompted Duke William of Normandy (William the Conqueror) to claim the throne of England upon the death of King Edward the Confessor in 1066. Remember also that Danish kings ruled England for much of the first half of the eleventh century, strengthening Norse ties to the throne. The relationships among William, Normans, Norse, and England are terribly convoluted, and the unstable politics along with the intrigue of the English court made the land ripe for invasion.

In terms of spelling, the Frenchness of the Normans is far more important than their Viking heritage. For political purposes, the Normans spoke a variant of French, so the Norman Conquest meant that the French language—which for the most part had been about as influential as a warning label on a pack of cigarettes—was the language of England's ruling class. True, French had made some contributions to English before 1066. For instance, Edward the Confessor was raised in France and imported many Norman favorites to help rule England, and that favoritism brought a few French loanwords into the language of the elite. Still, the impact on English was relatively minute until William the Conqueror established a more complete Norman rule.

His conquest was so thorough that for many years the ruling class of England spoke Norman French, with some not deigning to learn the common English tongue at all. Especially important to the history of English spelling is the fact that most major documents, records, and official texts were in French. Gradually, the forces of linguistic change and human nature would once again prove how conquerors often fall victim to a slow assimilation into the culture of the conquered, but the French influence was so powerful that it continued throughout the Middle English period and beyond.

This process of linguistic change was a difficult one, and the early Middle English period in particular had growing pains. The language of the government, court, law, and religion would be dominated by Norman English, which was increasingly becoming distinct from mainland French. In fact, the Norman conquerors were increasingly thinking of themselves as Anglo-Norman, not as French at all. This Norman loss of French identity would culminate with the French capture of Normandy in 1204. English nobles often owned property in both England and Normandy, but after 1204 they had to choose which side of the channel they called home. In 1337, the differences between England and France would be so profound that they resulted in the Hundred Years War. Surprisingly, it would take Parliament until 1362 to decide that pleadings in courts of law should be conducted in English rather than French, and courts took even longer—until at least 1420—to obey. The delay possibly stemmed from the challenge of locating legal terms in English that would match their French counterparts. Even today, though, Parliament uses Anglo-Norman phrases to describe certain acts or bills, such as "La Reyne le vault" (royal assent for a public bill).

Anglo-Norman never became English. It really never evolved into anything at all. By the end of the Middle English era, the Anglo-Norman language was archaic because it was not a first language for anyone, just a formal or ritual language that had to be learned rather than acquired naturally. Before fading away, the Anglo-Norman language would have an enormous impact on the English language—even greater than the Scandinavian influence on Old English.

In particular, many English words of today began as loanwords from French (this is especially true of modern words consisting of more than one syllable). Loanwords are important to spelling because many reflect the spelling system of the language from which they were taken—or they are a hybrid spelling. Sometimes, they replaced an English word entirely, such as *crime* completely replacing *firen*. Other Old English words succumbing to a French counterpart include *andweard* (present), *gecnyrdnyss* (study), *geglengan* (to adorn). To our modern eye, it seems a blessing not to deal with such Old English spellings, but who knows how these words might have evolved and simplified over the centuries had it not been for French usurpers?

Frequently, a French term did not so much replace as *merge* with an English counterpart, or the loanword would take on a new meaning based on its use among the English. Originally, the French word *apareil* referred, for example, to any sort of thing that was prepared, but in Anglo-Norman (and, before long, in English) the term came to be *apparel*, referring only to clothes. Another adaptation is the very English word *gentleman*, which was created by adding French *gentle* with Old English *man*. At other times, Middle English would base a loanword on the French spelling but provide a different pronunciation. This is true of "*h* words" in English such as *honest* and *hour* that have declined to be pronounced with <h> as they were in French.

Given the context in which French was used (in the ruling circles), it is not surprising that many of our present words dealing with the military, law, government, and religion are Anglo-Norman in origin. Here are a few examples:

attorney	judge
baron	jury
captain	preach
clergy	prince
corporal	soldier
court	usurp
crime	verdict
duke	vestment
government	

English is quirky for a reason. I find it interesting how our English vocabulary is often a by-product of politics and class divisions. These factors can drive changes in a language just as much as logic does. Needless to say, politics and class divisions are not altogether logically consistent, so it is no wonder our language and spelling are not always consistent either. We see these issues in French loanwords of Middle English.

For instance, English commoners and servants would provide the meals for the Anglo-Norman rulers, so accordingly, the terms for most domestic animals are Anglo-Saxon, as seen with *cow, calf, deer, ox, sheep*, and *swine*. In contrast, the terms referring to the meats presented at the rulers' tables are Anglo-Norman, as seen with *beef, veal, venison, mutton*, and *pork*. Unlike earlier Vikings, neither the Anglo-Saxons nor the Normans considered it Christian to eat horses, so we have no term for horse meat, other than *horse meat*. The French eventually acquired a taste and a term for this dish, supposedly as a result of Napoleon's starving troops needing sustenance, yet neither

Americans nor English have found a need to borrow their word for horse meat—*cheval*.

The Norman rulers of England, in fact, had a great fondness for food and brought along their cooking preferences. French terminology must have been used to explain to cooks and servants how to cook according to the French sensibilities. Many cooking terms of today—including *baste*, *boil*, *fry*, and *sauce*—are based on French loanwords that first appeared in Middle English.

Today, we see not only these culinary loanwords but also the elitism inherent in the vocabulary of the kitchen. When visiting Waffle House, one would most certainly not "dine" upon the "chef's cuisine" (words eventually taken from French). One would merely be "eating" the "cook's food" (all derived from good ol' Old English).

How did the common people of Britain react to the second-class status English was becoming in their country? Records of these reactions are scant. Quite likely, many commoners and peasants were unaware of the changes occurring in the schools, courts, and government. Others were clearly unhappy. In a short poem that literary scholars refer to as the *First Worcester Fragment*, an anonymous poet of the late twelfth century put forth his sentiments. The first line speaks fondly of Anglo-Saxon teachers and religious leaders of preinvasion days. This tone changes considerably when the poet refers to their Norman replacements:

> These taught our people in English. Their light was not dim but shown brightly.
> Now that teaching is forsaken, the folk are lost.
> Now there is another people which teaches our folk,
> And many of our teachers are damned, and our folk with them.

I have presented this translation, taken from S. K. Brehe's careful analysis of the poem, in Modern English, but the anonymous poet's negativity toward "another people" has certainly not been lost in translation. The poet was not alone in resenting the changes in the language, education, and religion of England.

It is all too easy to exaggerate the "two-tier" or "us-against-them" language system of the Middle English era. The truth is that common people did occasionally draw on the Anglo-Norman vocabulary of the ruling class, who themselves were increasingly bilingual and able to communicate in the people's English as well as Anglo-Norman (if for no other reason than it made it easier to give orders). As a result, Middle English acquired French loanwords that do not clearly reflect Anglo-Norman elitism or Anglo-Saxon subservience—words such as *grape*, *bachelor*, *dandelion*, and *crescent*.

Amazingly, the borrowing or adaptation of French words was not impeded by the strife and wars between England and France. Even after the collapse of the Anglo-Norman dialect, English continued its love affair with French words, if not French people. Indeed, the borrowings seem to have increased dramatically from around 1250 to the end of the Middle English period, and loanwords increasingly came from various parts of France, not just the Normandy region. In the fourteenth century, French would be the source of numerous abstract terms that end in *-ant*, *-ence*, *-tion*, and *-ment*. Such words did not necessarily replace existing English words but would usually supplement them, allowing more specific or varied meanings to be used in English. Just as the Scandinavian tongue influenced English at a time when Vikings and Anglo-Saxons were cutting each other's throats, the French language would influence English spellings despite wars and strife between the two nations.

Trying to measure the number of French words we now use is like measuring how many cars are truly "American made." A car is made up of metal parts, plastics, chemicals, ores, and unreadable warranties that originate or are assembled all over the world. Every "French" word is itself a mixture of diverse languages and dialects, so it is hard to determine if a particular word is French in origin or should be traced back further to, say, Latin or Greek. As a result of the complex mixing of cultures and languages, it is impossible to know for sure where and how many words originated, especially with common terms such as *boy* and *girl* (we do know that, as late as 1300, *gyrle* referred to a child of either gender).

Nonetheless, we can safely assume a third of today's English terms are taken from French or Anglo-Norman, although some estimates put the figure at closer to 50 percent. It seems ironic that many French people today mourn the increase in the number of modern French words taken from English; perhaps they are merely reclaiming words that were once thoroughly French.

The French also helped English find a more stable way to form plurals. Old English did not have one particular method of turning singular nouns into plural forms. For example, the singular form of the Old English word for *ship* could be *scip* while the plural could be *scipu*. In contrast, the singular of *stone* could be *stan*, while the plural could be *stanas*.

This might seem a grammatical concern, not a spelling issue. Yet spelling in any language is always more difficult when a word changes shape depending on its function or meaning. Spelling is even more complicated when each word appears to have its own unique way of changing form, or when the spelling of one form is significantly different from another, as was often the case with singular and plural nouns in Old English. During Middle English, the French influence led to a simplification that in truth had already been under way, partly because of Scandinavian influence. As a result of these influences, *-s* and *-en* endings gradually became a tag team to indicate plurality of most words, with *-s* eventually winning out. Today, the words *children*, *brethren*, and *oxen* appear to be the sole remains of the *-en* marker. The triumph of *-s* took many years, however. Plurals such as *shoon* and *eyen* were used all the way up to early Modern English before the *-s* forms (*shoes* and *eyes*) shoved them aside.

The victory was not total. The older Germanic ways of forming plurals have been retained in several words dealing with fundamental aspects of rural life. Notice how such words tend to indicate plurality through a change in vowels rather than in final consonants:

goose	geese
louse	lice
man	men
mouse	mice
tooth	teeth

A few other modern words have a "zero" plural taken from Old and Middle English. That is, with a few words, the singular and plural forms look exactly the same, as with *deer* and *sheep*. Increasingly, both the zero plural and the *-s* plural forms of these words—such as *fish* and *fishes*—are considered acceptable. We see the same acceptance of *-s* forms of words taken more recently from other languages. To the dismay of many spelling and lexical purists, *radii* and *octopi* are becoming *radiuses* and *octopuses* (the latter is not a word to be said too quickly).

These complex relationships have resulted in a complex spelling system in English. Many of our current words are a hybrid, or mongrel if you see it that way. These words can be traced back to a peculiar Latin-based French dialect (Anglo-Norman) that merged into the Germanic-based language of old England. This Germanic tongue itself was a by-product of an Old English amalgamation of various Germanic dialects that were gradually mixed with Norse dialects, along with a smidgen of Latin. The unsystematic merging of these peoples and languages largely account for the complexity of our spelling system.

Scribes Gone Wild

In terms of spelling, another lasting holdover from Middle English involves the sometimes lowly but always important scribes of the period—literate clerks who wrote, copied, and translated countless documents for government, courts, royalty, churches, and schools. Generally, these scribes would write in French or Anglo-Norman, yet they would also write using the Middle English of the common people, especially as the period wore on. The scribes' spelling decisions would drastically affect spelling of their time and accordingly our own.

As a result of their French training or influence, the scribes owed no allegiance to Wessex. As I discussed earlier, the Wessex dialect and spelling conventions had emerged as the linguistic norm in Old English. In 1066, Wessex fell from grace as King Harold's banner fell at Hastings, and before long scribes had the liberty of using whatever dialect or spelling system they thought appropriate. Another complication was that the Catholic church of Rome, which had endorsed William the Conqueror, became an even more powerful force in England, meaning Latin replaced English in most religious documents. Scribes had increasingly little reason to use, much less master, the Wessex way of spelling. For many years, English simply was not sufficiently official or dignified to warrant scribes' really caring to adhere to a particular English standard. The real power seemed to be in Normandy or, later, the English courts of Anglo-Norman rulers.

Spelling once again cannot be divorced from politics. The reason why scribes initially did not bother with any sort of English standard for spelling was that there was a lack of a national English identity and central power—a problem compounded by the rise of feudalism during the Middle Ages. As more and more common people owed allegiance to a particular lord rather than to the English kingdom, there was less and less reason for anyone to adhere to a national standard for writing and spelling. These shifts in English politics and economics provide just one historical example of how language norms are tied to power holdings—to the class or group that has prestige, dominance, and control in a community.

So if Wessex spellings were no longer chic, what did guide scribes' decisions about spelling? To say the least, they saw no reason to stay with the status quo of Anglo-Saxon Wessex.

Keep in mind that English spelling has always reflected, to one degree or another, an attempt to mimic spoken English. When scribes did bother to copy a text in English rather than Latin or French, they would be inclined to use spellings that were reflected in the pronunciation of whatever dialect they deemed suitable, such as the dialect of their particular neck of the British woods. As a result, we now have a few oddities such as *won't*. This contraction derived from the dialect form of *will* used in one region, while *will* itself derived from a different region. This inconsistency is partially due to the range of variants there once was for *will* and *won't*. With the latter, these competing forms included *wynnot*, *woonot*, *wo'not*, *we'n't*, and the logical (but strange to us now) *willn't*.

Similarly, if scribes felt like modernizing the spelling or wording of documents originally written in older times, they would do so in whatever way they deemed fit. At times, the decisions were so arbitrary and spontaneous that even an individual scribe would not be consistent in the spelling of the same word within one document (not that anyone but a medieval scribe has been guilty of such an act). A few even dared to spoil the rhymes of Old English poems by changing the spelling to reflect what they considered a more contemporary pronunciation. For at least two hundred years after the Norman invasion, there would be no standard for Middle English spelling.

Apparently, wild scribes were running amok with English orthography.

The truth is, however, that the scribes' liberties with the language were not altogether detrimental. For one thing, they bought English some needed time. Previously, I mentioned that toward the end of the Old English period the spelling system was becoming fixed even though the pronunciation of English was still changing, meaning that the phonetic-based spelling system was not keeping pace with the spoken language. The scribes did not halt this process, but by not adhering to the Wessex standard (or any standard), they did give the written language a little more time to adjust. In other words, the scribes' liberties with English meant the conventions of spelling had more time to catch up with speech patterns.

Nor were the scribes always in disagreement about the changes needed in English. When scribes by and large did agree, their modifications would eventually translate into a positive effect on today's spelling. Especially important today is how the scribes updated the alphabet and spelling so that spellings would not reflect certain archaic speech patterns of older English. The pronunciation of Middle English is considerably less foreign to modern ears than Old English. Consequently, upgrading the spelling of some words to reflect the speech of Middle English would normally result in spellings that are more compatible with modern pronunciations.

To put it crudely, the scribes' efforts to create spellings that reflected speech resulted in spellings that are less weird than Old English. During most of the Old English period, for instance, the <f> and <v> sounds were not considered distinct; indeed, the Anglo-Saxons did not even have *v* in their alphabet. By the end of Old English, though, the <f> sound became more noticeably "voiced" in certain words—a sound created by vibrating one's voice box (as opposed to vibrating someone else's). That is, <f> eventually became pronounced as <v> in words such as *seofon* (*seven*). Old English spellers stayed faithful to the Wessex spelling and kept the letter *f* even when it stood for <v>. The Anglo-Norman scribes, not burdened by loyalty to Wessex or *f*, tended to update the spelling of such words by using *v*. As a result, Old English *drīfan* and *ofer* ultimately became the modern *drive* and *over*. Frequently, then, the scribes produced spellings that better resembled the use of <v> in spoken Middle English.

The scribes were, though, not consistent with *v*. Often, it was interchangeable with *u* and sometimes *w*. Even by Shakespeare's era of Early Modern English, the verb *revel* would be spelled *reuel*. Despite scribes' efforts to use *v* more consistently, we still see the odd historical relationship between *f* and *v* in irregular plurals such as *wiv̲e̲s̲* (*wi̲f̲e*) and *leav̲e̲s̲* (*lea̲f̲*).

Another example involves the way English had evolved so that other sounds were more common and important, such as the <ch> sound. Ideally, this often-used sound should have its own letter rather than being a coupling of two letters that do not logically culminate in <ch>, but we should be thankful medieval scribes recognized the existence of this sound. Toward the end of the twelfth century, they began using the letters *ch* to represent the sound we hear today in *church* or *chide*. Up to that time, *c* was used for both <k> and <ch> sounds. As strange as it might seem to us now, the two sounds were not considered all that different during much of the Old English period. It's bad enough that today *c* can stand for <s> or <k>

sounds, but imagine how much worse it would be if *c* could still carry the <ch> sound as well.

If you really want to be thankful, keep in mind that Romans used *c* to represent <g> as well as <k>. This all-purpose letter could have easily been the Swiss Army knife of the alphabet, yet the scribes were able to place some limits on this adjustable letter.

Other scribal changes have proved less beneficial for today's spellers. As noted, most scribes were Anglo-Norman or heavily encouraged by the ruling class to follow French (or, at times, Latin) norms that governed which letters can stand for certain sounds. In addition, English was not being taught in schools; French was. Because they had little guidance or education in terms of "proper" English spelling (an almost nonexistent concept at the time), scribes would fall back on what they were taught—*French* spelling and conventions. The letter *c* is again a good example. In older French, *c* became *s* when near vowels such as *e* and *i*. As a result, French loanwords such as *cellar* would be spelled with *c*, even though it was not normal for *c* to represent the <s> sound in English. Anglo-Norman scribes would erratically employ this sort of *c*—even in English words predating the invasion. Hence, we now have *mice*, although *mouse* somehow retained its *s*.

The scribes didn't base their spellings solely on French preferences—they were not that systematic or single-minded. Being trained in Latin, the scribes would sometimes draw on the letter/sound relationships of that language. Most notably, they often used *o* to represent the short <u> sound, altering Old English spellings such as *cuman, sunu,* and *wulf* so that today we have *come, son,* and *wolf.*

But not all changes were based simply on French or even Latin habits.

In our modern age when even shopping lists can be word processed or printed off the Internet, we might forget the difficulties of reading handwritten documents. The typical medieval scribe certainly could not overlook this problem, and undoubtedly some changes in spelling occurred simply to make handwriting more readable to people whose long working days were composed of trying to read and write handwritten texts. One handwriting style popular during late Old English and early Middle English was the Carolingian script—a beautiful "font" with an emphasis on bold vertical strokes and rounding of the letters. Centuries before the Norman invasion, the French emperor Charlemagne himself endorsed this style of writing, so Anglo-Norman scribes in particular were fond of this script. Unfortunately, this bold style made certain letters difficult to distinguish from others. Consider the example of the chameleon-like *u* of the Old and early Middle English, a letter able to blend into its lexical environment and a major source of scribal eyestrain. In the Carolingian style (and even later styles such as the Gothic script), it was difficult to distinguish the letter *u* from an adjacent *m* or *n*. There were just too many "minims" in a row—too many vertical strokes of the pen, especially since many scribes preferred a claustrophobic style with letters placed extremely close to one another. The letter *u* was even more difficult to distinguish from a neighboring *v*. As a result of these assorted difficulties in recognizing the letter *u*, scribes used the letter *o* in such contexts to stand for *u*.

Today, the scribe's concern regarding *u* is no longer an issue. In handwritten as well as word-processed documents, we use styles of letters that make it reasonably clear when we are using an *m*, *n*, *u*, or *v*. We no longer see any benefit of the scribes' solution to their problem, only the illogical results. English still has many words that use *o* to make the short <u> sound, but typically this phenomenon occurs only when *m*, *n*, or *v* are in close proximity, as in *love, monkey, some, ton, tongue*, and *woman*. I say "illogical," but it is almost always the case that there is in fact a logic behind an irregular spelling, as in the case of *o* that wants to be *u*. The problem is that the logic is no longer evident or meaningful in our scribe-deprived world.

Thankfully, medieval scribes found other ways to distinguish letters from one another. The lowercase version of the letter *i* was once confused with the vertical strokes of letters such as *m* and *n*. The problem was that the lowercase version was the merest wisp of a letter—a short vertical line with no dot hovering above it. In this situation, the solution for many scribes was to add this little dot to create present-day *i*, thereby distinguishing the letter from almost all others. In fact, the name of the dot is *tittle*, which is derived from a Latin term referring to a sign or marker.

Once again, though, scribes did not always communicate well with one another, so many used *y* instead of *i* as a way of helping the letter stand apart from a nearby *m* or *n*. Others— probably in the days before the tittle was considered as a solution—used *o* instead of *i*, and thus *wimen* became *women*. (Ironically, *wimen* is sometimes used today by writers who want to indicate that somebody speaks with a backward accent, as in "Bubba said, 'I kissed me some wimen today.'" The irony is *wimen* is not a peculiar pronunciation at all; it might look ignorant, but it reflects the way most people correctly pronounce the word.)

The Middle English scribes also tidied up the alphabet by retiring certain letters, even though it would take centuries for the changes to become truly standard. The reasons behind the scribes' cleansing of the alphabet are complex and not altogether understood today, but it is clear that one major reason is the Anglo-Norman scorn for non-Roman letters (keep in mind that the French language and script were more directly derived from the Roman language). Five major letters were replaced, all having their roots in Old English and not taken directly from the old Roman alphabet. As a whole, the removal of the five letters was positive for modern spelling. The problem is that English writers had been particularly inconsistent in terms of what sounds these letters represented. Eventually, these five letters would be replaced by more stable letters.

One of the first to go was the letter ash (*ae*), which began disappearing around 1100. Another was one of two surviving Germanic runes: wynn, which around 1300 would become *w* after scribes tried a prototype consisting of two *u*'s (as in "double-u").

The least understood reject is yogh, which looks something like the numeral three (3). A version of yogh was used in Old English, yet later it would represent a range of sounds made at the back of the upper mouth, such as the <g> sound. French scribes would eventually replace yogh with *g* or, at times, *gh*. The yogh would stay around for years to stand for one sound or another, as if it were willing to play any position just to stay on the alphabetic team. The desperate yogh was so erratically used that we are better off without it, although it loitered in Scotland until the late fourteenth century.

Modern spelling would be closer to the "one-letter, one-sound" ideal if two other letters had survived in some form: eth (ð) and thorn (þ). Both would eventually be replaced by *th*, but the eth and thorn sounds are as different as *f* and *v*. In general, eth was voiced (as in *then*), while thorn—which was taken from the rune alphabet—was unvoiced (as in *thin*). Neither of these sounds has its own letter in our modern alphabet, and to make it worse, the same combination of letters (*th*) is used now to represent these distinct sounds. The Norman scribes must have known that for centuries eth and thorn had been used inconsistently to distinguish the voiced and voiceless <th> sounds, so apparently they decided to clean house by banishing both wayward letters.

Well, not entirely. The exile of these letters was gradual, especially in terms of thorn (þ). For some reason, *the* was particularly eager to hold onto its thorn.

When the printing press was invented, printers did not keep a thorn in their stock of letters, for it had all but disappeared. Instead, early printers used what they considered a suitable visual (but not phonetic) alternative: the letter *y*. The result is *ye*, as in "ye olde Macintosh computer." Contrary to popular belief, this type of *ye* was never pronounced in the Old or Middle English with the <y> sound. We find this pronunciation only in Modern English, when people think they are cleverly speaking Old or Middle English.

During medieval times, however, one type of *ye* was pronounced with the <y> sound. It was a plural form of *you* similar in meaning to the Southern *y'all*, as with "Oh come, all ye [y'all] faithful." This *ye* is another linguistic feature that found final refuge in Scotland, where it can occasionally still be heard. (As a few people might recall, there was also the yé-yé style of music in 1960s France. The phrase "yé-yé" is peculiarly derived from English but has nothing to do with *the* or *you*; it is based instead on what French teenagers assumed to be the customary way to end British pop music, as in "I love you . . . yeah, yeah, yeah." Yé-yé music is best forgotten, although it illustrates how linguistic and cultural contributions eventually sailed both ways across the Channel.)

Sounds of Silence and Other Effects of Speech

Runes might have been carved in stone, but that did not keep them or other alphabets from changing. To understand our spelling system, we must realize that for centuries the Roman alphabet used in Britain was not a settled matter, largely because English has its roots in Germanic languages that the Roman alphabet was never designed to cover. The alphabet on which even the Roman alphabet was based has a complex history of its own and is not as stable as people tend to believe.

John Man describes the origins of "the" alphabet in *Alpha Beta: How 26 Letters Shaped the Western World*. Our modern English alphabet can be traced back to Latin and Greek alphabets that developed between approximately 500 B.C. and 750 B.C. The author argues that the real credit for all phonetic alphabets goes back much earlier, to the fourth millennium B.C. in Mesopotamia, where a crude phonetic alphabet was developed, apparently to keep records for trade and commerce. The notion that writing might be based on sounds rather than ideograms or even syllables was a surprisingly novel idea for hundreds of years, and it took many centuries for the concept to spread to other parts of the world. Along the way, the alphabet was adopted and refined by various peoples: the Egyptians, whose writing did not rely exclusively on hieroglyphic "pictures" or icons; Phoenician traders, whose alphabet bears resemblance to what we use today; the Greeks, who incorporated more vowels into the alphabet; the mysterious Etruscans of central Italy; and then the Romans, who lent their name to an alphabet that would be adopted by most of the Europe they conquered and controlled.

One version or another of this Roman alphabet has long been the basis of written English. The key word is *version*—for a few letters went in and out of the alphabet for centuries, especially in Old English. Much later, the printing press helped put a stop to such nonsense. But the whole of Britain was not always using the same version for much of Old English and even some of Middle English. Most of the differences involved only a few letters such as the yogh and thorn.

These alphabetic discrepancies were sometimes due to scribes' biases and preferences, yet at other times they were related to changes going on in common speech of an era (as with the aforementioned Danish or Norman influences). There were so many linguistic changes going on in a sporadically unified England that the alphabet, the spelling of words, and spoken pronunciations were destined not to be in sync. Spelling in particular lagged behind changes in the speech of England, while the alphabet was even slower.

Consider another example of how changes in speech affected spelling. Old English frequently made use of sounds rarely heard in Modern English. One such sound is the "rough" <ch> sound we sometimes hear today in *loch*. The yogh letter often represented this sound, so it should not be surprising that the sound is still heard in Scotland, where yogh was last seen. In Middle English, *gh* would eventually be used to represent this sound, but by the end of the period, this noise would be as much of a presence in England as the Loch Ness Monster, which is negligible seeing as how Nessie has long been hidden in Scottish waters.

Although this sound is rarely heard today, we still "see" the old pronunciation of *gh* in words such as *knight* (the *k* was also pronounced). The silent *gh* in Modern English is the fossilized remains of what was once an important sound; the spelling just could not keep up with the changes in speech. The *gh* is usually silent, but sometimes—perhaps because the old yogh stood for so many sounds over the centuries—it represents the <f> sound in a few words that end in *gh*. Here are a few examples of the silent and *f*-like *gh*:

bright	might
brought	sigh
caught	sight
cough	though
laugh	tough

Most silent letters of today were once pronounced (the silent *e* is so important today that I will reserve a discussion of it for later). One interesting example that does not receive much attention involves *b*. In Middle English speech, the <b> sound usually became lost after the <m> sound, yet spelling was already becoming fixed. Words such as *lamb* and *climb* now have a silent *b* where it was once pronounced.

Can we claim *b* is *always* silent in words containing *mb*? You already know the answer. Only rarely can we use the word *always* when describing modern spelling. Still, the exceptions are not completely arbitrary. Not all "*mb* words" have a silent *b*, because Middle English actually *added* the <b> sound to a few Old English words, especially when *m* was followed by the <l>, <r>, or <n> sound. Therefore, we do indeed have the <b> sound in "*mb*" words such as *nimble*. The *b* is also pronounced in loanwords such as *resemble*, which came into Middle English by way of French.

Another speech change resulting in silent letters involves <w>. By the end of Middle English, speakers often dropped this sound when it appeared right after the <s> or <t> sound. The spelling of some words would reflect this change by likewise dropping the letter *w* after *s* or *t*, yet a few other words stubbornly kept the silent *w* (as in *sword*). Keep in mind there was no law mandating that the <w> sound had to be abolished. Language change is based on what people prefer, so there are few universal rules, just as there are relatively few universal preferences.

Put another way, linguistic evolution is not like the rigorously logical world of mathematics. Language change is a mechanism that literally operates by word of mouth, so it is a slow, uneven process. We have to understand that, because our system of spelling has long been an attempt to represent spoken sounds, spelling is directly affected by larger linguistic principles and changes, especially those dealing with speech. Linguistic change and spelling are like a story that is repeated orally over decades, with quirky changes made along the way and with some parts being added or deleted depending on who is doing the telling. As a result of this messy process, only at our peril should we attempt to form rigid rules for spelling.

We see this messiness in the <w> example. Several words— such as *swallow* and *twin*—maintained both the letter *w* and the

<w> sound, even though the sound is preceded by <s> or <t>. Sometimes, the sound would disappear and then return years later, perhaps because the spelling kept the *w* and people figured they had better pronounce it.

Toward the end of the Middle English period, the last significant change in English pronunciation took place: the Great Vowel Shift. The specifics of what happened are complex, but the overall effect was that the pronunciation of several vowels changed considerably. Before the shift, English speakers would consider certain vowel sounds far more significant than we do now. These sounds to us merely seem to be taking a longer time to be pronounced. However, for many English people who lived before 1400, the length of time it took to utter a vowel could turn it into what they considered to be an entirely different vowel. These "long vowels" were not simply dropped during the Great Vowel Shift; they were replaced. For example, the vowel we hear in *mouse* was once pronounced like *oo* in *moose*. Some of the older pronunciations can still be heard in Scotland (such as saying <hoose> for the word *house*).

Many of these vowel changes had been under way since the thirteenth century, while a few would not become widespread until the eighteenth. During 1400 to 1450, though, the vowel shift accelerated to the point where you could have distinctly heard the pronunciation differences in two generations of the same family. The changes did not occur systematically, which at least partially accounts for the different pronunciations of *oo* in *mood*, *blood*, and *good*. In general, the most commonly used words tend to be the first to succumb to changes in speech such as the Great Vowel Shift. The trend is often the opposite with spelling, with frequently used words being particularly resistant to being respelled.

As I will discuss in the next chapter, spelling was increasingly standardized beginning in the 1400s, so—as we have seen before—standardization occurred while major changes in speech were still in progress (this time, the Great Vowel Shift). As a result, speech was again changing while spelling was not keeping up, creating numerous spellings that today seem odd. The Great Vowel Shift greatly affected speech, but the changes did not carry over to most spellings. When spellings were modified to reflect such changes, often the changes were not consistently applied. The combination *-ough* is one victim of written discourse lagging behind speech, as seen in the different ways it is pronounced in *rough*, *through*, *though*, *trough*, and *plough*.

Middle English included many other consonant and vowel changes, some of which affect spelling. But my point is not to catalog all of these transformations but to provide examples of larger issues and explanations of why our spelling system seems illogical at times. By now, it should be abundantly clear that the difficulties of English spelling are usually the result of changes in speech. Not only was it difficult for the written language to keep up with the complex and not always consistent changes in speech, but the changes were sometimes handled differently across the land. For most of its history, Britain lacked a true standard or set of conventions for both writing and speech.

It should also be clear why there was no English standard during much of Old and Middle English: the kingdom was not sufficiently unified itself, often as a result of one people or another successfully invading and taking charge.

But why were there so many changes in English speech — or why does any spoken language change at all for that matter? The reasons behind changes in speech, such as consonants becoming silent, are too many to discuss thoroughly here, but one major reason is that people adjust their language whenever there are notable, lasting transformations in the power structure or population of a land — as seen with changes wrought by Anglo-Saxon tribes, Vikings, Normans, and even missionaries who brought Christianity to Britain. This ebb and flow of various languages and dialects into and within the region significantly affected spoken English.

You can see similar effects at a much smaller level when individuals "style shift" their pronunciation and word choices based on the language of whoever seems to be listening. If you grew up having a regional accent and later moved to another part of the country, you likely style shift without being fully aware how you are taking on bits and pieces of the dialect that now surrounds you — unaware, that is, until folks back home let you know you are starting to "talk funny" (note the suspicion in their voice, as if you have become a traitor). This sort of dynamic works both ways. When I lived in northwest America, people talking to me would often become embarrassed when they started using *y'all* or pronouncing words with a drawn-out Texas twang, such as pronouncing *ham* as two syllables (<ha-em>). My friends were afraid I thought they were mocking me (which I'm sure was the case at times), but usually I just thought they were talking normal for once.

In similar ways, diverse speech patterns within a nation will reflect, to one extent or another, the speech habits of immigrants, the influx of foreign powers, or the redistribution of internal power holdings so that one region's dialect is considered the most prestigious (as with Wessex, for a while).

Speech undergoes change for other reasons, and many theories have developed about why and how speech evolves, some having more credibility than others. Despite what people too often believe, dialects are not connected at all with hot or cold weather, so any temperature change in England has nothing to do with changes in English dialects.

While it might sound just as far fetched at first, one theory holds that the black plague explains many changes in the language of Britain. During the midfourteenth century, thousands of peasants and workers died because of the plague, which ironically increased the value of the lower socioeconomic class—or at least those who survived. As noted earlier, the prestige of any language or dialect is directly related to power and prestige of the people using this language variety. Accordingly, the increased esteem given to common people meant their common language was more acceptable. In 1349, in fact, everyday English began to be used in English schools again, eventually replacing Latin even though classical languages would long remain a fundamental part of what was considered a good education (the term "grammar school" derives from the teaching of Latin or Greek grammar, not English).

The dialects of the farms, streets, and markets thus influenced what would emerge as Standard English. Perhaps the true hallmark of Middle English is that during this period the status of English went from an abrupt fall to a gradual, steady recovery. Even though the English language itself was slowly being rehabilitated during Middle English's watch, this period is not credited with the establishment of a particular standard for English, which is a prerequisite for any spelling system. That credit goes to Modern English, which most scholars say began with the sixteenth century.

English speech before 1500 was in many ways like a stew in which fresh ingredients were constantly being added—new cultural, historical, and maybe even biological ingredients that did not always readily combine. Eventually, all of these came together in a messy way to produce Modern English, along with our standard conventions for spelling. These conventions would have been more logical today had it not been for the tumultuous events occurring during the Old and Middle English period. However, we would be poorer in other ways had not these same events caused a rich mixing of diverse cultures and ideas.

The forces that shaped spelling did not end with Middle English. Modern English saw the rise of a national standard for the language, yet this period also contributed its own idiosyncrasies to our spelling system.

The Return of the King's English

On January 1, 1500, everyone abruptly stopped speaking Middle English.

Well, not quite. Determining the time frame for a linguistic period is not a science. Setting a date for the beginning of Modern English is especially challenging. The withdrawal of Rome from Britain left a benchmark for the beginnings of Old English, while the Norman Conquest provided the same for Middle English. Yet no famed historical event is credited with launching Modern English.

The transition from Middle to Modern English was also particularly slow. In fact, historical linguists frequently use the phrase "Early Modern English" to describe the language of 1500 to 1800, when many changes were in the works. In 1500, the Great Vowel Shift was very much in progress, and a few consonants were still in the process of being dropped in speech, leading to more silent letters in spelling.

For instance, the <l> sound was sometimes lost in spoken words yet retained in their written counterparts, as with *walk* and *talk* (some people pronounce this sort of *l*, so they detect no silence at all in these words). The <k> and <g> sounds in words starting with *kn* or *gn* did not disappear until nearly 1700, leaving the spellings *knight*, *knave*, and *gnat* in the wake of this change. The <w> sound in words starting with *wr* also took time to disappear, resulting in spellings such as *write* (try pronouncing this *w*—it seems unnatural to us now).

During Early Modern English, the number of words in English more than doubled, largely as a result of loanwords from Latin, Greek, and French. Such changes affected spelling, but relatively few major changes in terms of the entire English language were made after the end of Early Modern English.

Nonetheless, most linguists and historians agree the year 1500 is a reasonable choice to mark the beginnings of our Modern English, not because of the English Renaissance, which started around 1520, but because of something less grand—the increasing prestige of the London dialect. No study of spelling is complete without understanding how this idiom went from being a second-class dialect to becoming the model for formal English, written and spoken.

London Emerges

London was (and still is) home to several dialects, but one became the basis of what we now refer to as Standard English, from which we derive modern spelling. Some people are not enthused about words such as *standard*, with its connotations of stifling sameness and anti-individuality. These same people are probably among the millions, though, who are annoyed with English spelling, which would be less irritating if spelling rules were truly standardized.

The standardization of written English is, in other words, a vital aspect of spelling. Although English spelling might not be as consistent as we might prefer, standardization in the past five hundred years has made spelling far less chaotic and irregular than it would have become otherwise. London ways of speaking and writing provided a much-needed template for an English standard. Today, especially in America, we are not aware that English dialects of the Middle Ages were more distinct than they are now. (We often think the English have always spoken like either the queen or street urchins such as Oliver Twist.) During the first half of the Middle English period, the northern and southern dialects of Britain were particularly different from one another—not just with commoners but with all classes of people. In addition to providing standards for writing, the London norm helped bring these diverse dialects closer together, promoting easier communication without losing dialects altogether.

We have to go surprisingly far back to determine who planted the seeds of the London standardization. William the Conqueror, though he wreaked havoc on much of England in 1066, saw the economic and political value of sparing London. He helped turn it into a greater commercial city, with its citizens enjoying considerable rights and privileges. Soon thereafter, London displaced Winchester as the political center of England.

But London was still not the *linguistic* center of England. After the invasion, English was denigrated as a sort of peasant language. In London and the whole of England, French and Latin would long remain the primary languages for political, legal, government, and religious writing and speech.

Eventually the dialect of the London region would become the standard, but we surely cannot claim it was a result of London being the capital. To the say the least, a nation's capital is never the only choice as a model for speech or writing in a language—Washington, DC, being a prime example. No one reason led to the rise of the London standard.

London's claim as home of the linguistic as well as royal throne was assisted by demographics. The larger region of East Midland, which contributed the basis of what would become the London standard, emerged by late Middle English as the most populous area of Britain. One advantage of the East Midland dialect was its "moderateness" in that it was not extremely different from other English dialects. By 1400, the London dialect, as influenced by East Midland, was becoming increasingly prestigious. The written form of this dialect gained another boost because the most famous writer of that era, Chaucer, used the East Midland dialect. (People tend to exaggerate the influence of literary writers on the development of English; truth be told, the medieval equivalent of technical writers had far more influence.)

These features of London were not enough for its dialect to become the standard form of English. Not only were there rival dialects, but English itself was still suffering from centuries of being viewed as an inferior language. As discussed earlier, people are inherently snobbish about what they deem as inappropriate or improper language, and it was not easy for the English populace to change strongly held perceptions of their own native tongue. It is difficult for a language to develop a standard when the language itself has long been considered substandard.

Earlier, I suggested the year 1500 is a somewhat arbitrary date for the launch of Modern English. My own belief is that 1400 is more appropriate because, without question, the 1400s saw English return as a language worthy of kings as well as commoners. True, the literary elite, scholars, and clergy would be among the last to recognize vernacular English as being a worthy mechanism for their discourses; most balked until at least the latter half of the sixteenth century. Nevertheless, political and social events of the fifteenth century led London Eng-

lish to become a bona fide means of communication throughout most of England.

Perhaps more than anything else, what helped London
become the standard for writing and spelling occurred around
1420. At that time, English officially and in practice became
the written language of the royal administrative offices known
as the Chancery, housed in the London area (more specifically,
in the city of Westminster). The written form of English was
thus standardized before the spoken form. Chancery English
was not truly a new dialect, and it introduced relatively few
new spellings. Chancery scribes instead drew on existing
spellings and grammatical choices, especially those found in
London.

The impact was far reaching, not only in royal matters but
in all of government. Court records, appeals, deeds, petitions,
legislative proceedings—all these and more were to be written
in English. This move had been underfoot for years and had
precedence in Parliament, but by 1423 Chancery scribes
adopted a dialect within London as the norm for their writing.
With regard to official writing, this style—nowadays called
Chancery English—would soon be recognized across the
realm as the official standard, displacing French and Latin in
most formal contexts.

While English had been gradually gaining on French and
Latin in importance prior to 1400, English might have leap-
frogged ahead because of the shrewdness of two kings. John
H. Fisher, author of *The Emergence of Standard English*, argues
that the development of English as the norm stemmed directly
from political maneuverings of Henry IV and his son Henry V,
both of whom were struggling to retain power during their
reigns (approximately 1413 to 1471). To obtain what they
needed, these two kings were obliged to appeal to the common
people of England, especially given the increasing powers of

Parliament. The consequence is that father and son emphasized common English, rather than French or Latin. Henry V, in fact, would be the first king since the Norman Conquest to use English regularly in his official writings.

Even a monarch must turn to "the little guy" to get the job done. One final time, scribes would be the instruments of linguistic change. Especially important to spelling is that government and royal scribes were a close-knit group, able to communicate quickly and frequently with one another about spelling and other writing problems or questions. Housed in London, they formed the critical mass of influential agents of change needed to move English toward a standard. Outside the halls of government and court, the Chancery style would be imitated by merchants, printers, and community leaders who wanted to associate themselves with the language of power and influence.

By 1500, English had again become the official as well as the vernacular language of choice, and Chancery English of London became His Majesty's orthographical flagship. With its emphasis on learning, the English Renaissance along with the continued rise of the middle class led to a huge increase in the number of children receiving formal education, so spellings pouring out of the clerical offices of London were being fixed in the minds of thousands of students.

As the sixteenth century progressed, there would be signs of an English backlash against the French and the French language in general. William Shakespeare's plays reflect this reaction. Sometimes Shakespeare's attitude is subtle, sometimes very direct. In *Henry V*, he has Henry V proclaim to Princess Katherine: "Fie upon my false French! By mine honor, in true English, I love thee." In such ways, Shakespeare would connect the French culture and language with dishonesty, ridiculousness, and prissiness.

Beware, though, of adopting an "either/or" theory of language development. The influence of French and Latin most certainly did not stop in 1500. If anything, their influence on English actually increased, albeit as a support system for English rather than its replacement. In government, especially with regard to legal matters, hundreds of French and classical terms were incorporated into English so this "fledgling" language could better describe judicial, bureaucratic, and business ideas that had been the domain of French and Latin. If these other languages were training wheels of sorts, they never came off. Most foreign loanwords found in Early Modern English are still with us.

As I mentioned before, loanwords are not just a matter of vocabulary. A loanword to some extent reflects the spelling used in the original language—even when retaining the original spelling creates inconsistencies.

For instance, in the French of this period, *ch* tended to reflect the <sh> sound. French loanwords such as *chaperon* used this same *ch* spelling, although a few English writers tried to begin the word more logically with the letters *sh*. By drawing on the French preferences for letters and sounds, the Brits added a second function for *ch* when it was allowed to stand for <sh> (another French loanword of this sort is *chef*). Earlier in Middle English, *ch* was primarily reserved for the <ch> sound heard in *church*. The multitasking of *ch* did not stop with <sh> and <ch>. Another major chore for *ch* would be added when Latin- and Greek-based words such as *chronology* and *charisma* made their way into Modern English, adding the <k> sound associated with *ch* in Greek. As a result of these additions to the lexicon, today *ch* makes the traditional <ch> sound about 62 percent of the time, <k> some 26 percent, and <sh> about 12 percent, according to a large-scale study published in 1970 by linguist and literacy expert Dr. Richard Venezky. Not all of these <k> and <sh> words came into being in early Modern English (the secular meaning of *charismatic*, for instance, was not introduced until the 1920s), but these percentages still indicate the way French and classical loanwords flooded into our language during this period.

Throughout the Renaissance, scholars and educators were in fact rediscovering ancient classical Western cultures. As a result, Greek and Latin loanwords poured into English. Many, such as *pneumatic* and *psychology*, have silent letters that were pronounced in the classical tongue but created unusual pronunciations for the British. The silent letters were maintained simply because they made classical etymology more apparent. Often, even words that had been in English for many years were updated to make them at least look more Greek or Latin, a move guaranteeing troublesome spellings.

Take, for instance, our Modern English word *scissors*. It is derived from Middle English *sisoures*, but in the 1500s, *sc-* was needlessly added just to make the word resemble the Latin term *scindere* (to split). However, this is *not* the root word of *scissors* at all.

Usually, the reformed spellings of the Renaissance were based on more accurate, if still imprudent, logic. A guiding principle of this early attempt to reform English spelling was that, when deemed appropriate, the spelling of words should reflect their classical etymology—their Latin or Greek roots in particular. Some people now argue these revisions were a way of ennobling English in an aesthetic sense. Some claim the spelling reforms were made in hopes that English would more accurately communicate important ideas if the classical root words were more evident. And still others say the reforms were simply a way to make literacy particularly accessible for the nobles and intellectual elite, most of whom were still well versed in Latin or Greek. Whatever the reasons, the Renaissance encouraged a classical reform of spelling, resulting in many words having a more Latin and Greek appearance.

Again, the results were not always positive in terms of spelling today. For example, *debt* comes from Middle English *det* or *dette*. These two older words were taken from the French, who themselves had borrowed from Latin *debita*. Although silent and useless now, *b* was added in Early Modern English just so the Latin etymology would be more apparent. Similarly, Middle English *samon* became *salmon* to show its classical roots, despite the silent *l*.

Many other words—including *island*, *indict*, *aisle*, *scythe*, *receipt*, and *victuals*—were more logically spelled *before* their spelling was changed to make them appear etymologically stylish. Spelling reforms can actually make matters worse, a lesson worth remembering.

Power of the Olive Press

When people look at spelling from a historical perspective, they often make the mistake of going straight to the invention of the printing press and the way it supposedly stabilized or "froze" our spelling system. Lore has it that English printers, having had enough of the chaos of spelling, brought law and order by using their trusty printing presses to mass produce the spellings they deemed best. Similar lore has it that the publication of the King James Bible and Shakespeare's plays heralded orthographic stability into English in order to preserve the beauty and power of these texts, but stabilization was already under way when the works appeared in the early 1600s. Nor did these texts reflect the range of spellings that were modified during Early Modern English.

As discussed already, the standardization of spelling is primarily the result of Chancery scribes who, employing simpler technology, preceded their heirs to the manuscript trade by several decades. Giving printers the credit (or blame) for standardizing spelling is like saying steelworkers designed New York skyscrapers. Chancery scribes, intentionally or not, were the architects and engineers of our spelling system. The printers did the important work of finishing and refining the work the scribes started. The construction of modern English spelling, however, begins with these scribes.

Now, though, it is time to consider how the printing press influenced spelling. Historians do not agree on the extent to which printers affected our spelling system, but all agree the invention of the printing press influenced orthography in diverse ways, even though it took years before their impact was broadly felt.

Johannes Gutenberg, a German goldsmith, usually receives credit for inventing the printing press around 1450, but the truth is he took ideas that had existed for centuries and improved upon them. In fact, his first press was essentially an olive oil press he had modified. Even movable type had been around for centuries in eastern Asia. In 1234, the world's first movable metal type had been used in Korea to publish a text whose title we would now translate as *Prescribed Ritual Texts of the Past and Present*. Gutenberg improved movable type and other parts of the press, resulting in a practical method of casting each letter or character onto its own piece of metal. Before Gutenberg's press, a European printer would usually have to rub an impression by using wood on which images and text had been carved—a laborious, time-consuming task.

Considering how the technology needed for a printing press had long been in existence before 1450, why didn't it develop sooner in Europe? Perhaps the answer rests with the refinements Gutenberg made to existing tools and methods, but his major contribution might relate more to economics than technology. He made it clear that mass printing could be financially profitable, especially as a result of the gradual but steady increase in literacy and commerce throughout Europe. Gutenberg himself went bankrupt, mostly because of a lawsuit and his personal spending habits. However, people across Europe realized his press could be financially viable. The demographics and economics were finally right, then, for mass production of texts.

The European printing press caught the eye of a well-traveled Englishman named William Caxton. In 1476, he brought the first true printing press to Britain, but a positive impact on spelling was still years away. For one thing, the quality of writing, editing, and typesetting was often shaky in England, unlike the quality found in the rest of Europe. Other factors kept the early printing press of England from being the orthographical force it would become later. Presses certainly did not blossom overnight in the British Isles. Even by 1500, only a handful of English presses were producing books in any quantity.

True, the printed books that did appear were mass produced, and one would think hundreds of copies of a given text would help "teach" a particular spelling to the reading public, just as one might assume this new industry would prefer regular ways of spelling in order to make typesetting more efficient and less debatable. But such was not the case until roughly a century after Caxton brought the press to England. Early printers in Britain did not communicate with one another as did Chancery scribes. These first printers as a whole did not adhere to the Chancery standard, nor any particular English standard at all. A few influential presses did not even publish their books in English. The press established in 1478 at Oxford focused on scholarship and refrained from publishing in English for decades.

Caxton and his fellow printers are not easy to categorize. Some historians have characterized Caxton as being interested only in selling books and making money. Others have portrayed him as a savior who almost single-handedly rescued English orthography from pandemonium. Neither extreme is true of course. The early printers of Britain were a diverse mixture of individuals, and even each individual printer had varied goals and assumptions about printing, English, and standardization.

These early printers cared about the English language, yet their backgrounds and motivations varied in terms of preparing them for any sort of literary or orthographic crusade. This variation is part of the reason why standardizing spelling was not a high priority for most printers. For example, William Caxton and most other printers did not receive the careful training in the finer points of writing as did Chancery scribes, but Caxton was certainly educated enough to translate several books into English. He printed many works based on public demand, yet he was also fond of publishing literary works he himself admired. Until later in the sixteenth century, the first printers did not pay great attention to linguistic developments or what came out of the Chancery or Parliament, yet they were not ignorant either of ongoing changes in English. Around 1480, Caxton wrote: "And certaynly our langage now used varyeth ferre from that whiche was used and spoken when I was borne." Although he was aware of standard spellings emerging in London, his own spelling of certain words varied considerably, indicating he did not see a great need for regularity in spelling.

Caxton usually relied on employees who, like his equipment, were not English, and their typesetting and spellings sometimes reflected foreign preferences and conventions. Caxton's press is credited with one infamous glitch still present in our spelling: the use of *gh* for the <g> sound in *ghost* and *ghastly* (apparently, the latter was changed because it was erroneously considered related to *ghost*). At the time, *gh* was the correct spelling choice—in Dutch. The continental influence made itself felt in other ways. Often overlooked in histories of English printing is the fact that foreign printing houses, such as those in Belgium and France, published many books for English readers, and their spellings indicate the publishers' command of English—Chancery English in particular—was occasionally lacking.

The reliance on foreign technology did not always result in spelling inconsistencies. Printers helped put a final end to a letter that had been hanging around for centuries—the runic thorn (þ). In England of the 1400s, few people and even fewer words used the uncharismatic thorn, which once had the potential to distinguish the "soft" <th> sound from its voiced <th> counterpart. The printers' European-made equipment did not include this letter, because it was not used much outside the British Isles. Thus, English printers replaced the thorn with *th* or, as I mentioned in a previous chapter, with *y*.

Another peculiarity of the early English press, one which did not vanish until well into the seventeenth century, was that typesetters would occasionally alter spellings just so the word length would create a justified right-side margin. Some misspellings, in other words, were intentionally used to create a prettier margin. To be fair, the typesetters usually reserved such changes for words that, at least in their mind, had more than one legitimate spelling, such as using the variant *doe* for *do*.

Not until the midsixteenth century would a substantial number of English printers regularly use the standardized spelling system—the one created by Chancery scribes more than a hundred years earlier. It would take longer, into the early 1600s, for such printers to make a substantial impact on the spelling of the general public. By that time, several influential textbooks and treatises on spelling, most notably Richard Mulcaster's *Elementarie* of 1582, had been published and significantly influenced not only printers but teachers and their students as well. As seen at other times in the development of English, though, standardization occurred when the spoken language was still evolving, meaning that spellings established in the Modern English period would often reflect older pronunciations.

Peace at Last?

We have been looking at more than a thousand years of spelling history, and it should be clear by now that these were not stable times for English spelling, not to mention British culture, politics, and society in general.

So it might seem surprising to realize how quickly changes in spelling subsided after 1700. By this time, the press had finally helped propagate Chancery English as a standard, the major pronunciation shifts in spoken English had largely been completed, and English itself was no longer seen as a second-class language, just as Great Britain itself had emerged as a major power around the globe (symbolically reflected in the official adoption of the name "Kingdom of Great Britain" in 1707). Not coincidentally, the early 1700s saw the beginning of a great stream of English words into languages around the globe, including those that for centuries had loaned their words to Old and Middle English.

Although many history-making events and social changes would occur after 1700, English spelling had at last found a "consistency foothold" that made massive changes in spelling unlikely. That is, by this time, there were widely accepted rules and conventions for spelling based on London preferences. The literate population of Great Britain and colonies such as America had finally embraced the simple notion that consistency in English spelling is a good thing.

This latter point—the establishment of a consistency foothold for English—cannot be emphasized enough. Today, we take it as a given that a spelling system should produce stable, consistent spellings. Until the 1700s, however, English-speaking people usually did not perceive a great need for stabilization in spelling, especially during previous centuries when English was considered too vulgar a language to ever have a logical system of spelling. Nor until the last few hundred years has there been a sufficiently powerful sense of national identity in Britain for there to be enough literate people to promote a systematic approach to English. Such prejudices are hard to dispel when handed down through generations. As did many writers of the Elizabethan period (1558 to 1603), even Shakespeare would spell the same words inconsistently. For instance, he supposedly used both *wrinkle* and *wrinckle* (although it is not certain he actually produced the spellings found in manuscripts of his plays), and for many years Shakespeare's own name would be spelled in various ways.

The reputation of English and the appreciation of consistency in spelling increased quickly during the seventeenth century. Only a few major changes were made to British spellings after 1700, and even these were generally limited to individual words rather than large-scale alterations. One significant change was solidifying our alphabet. Even at this late date, it was still not completely firm, though the thorns had finally been plucked out. The letters *u* and *j* took time to be widely recognized in England as being distinct from *v* and *i*. Other late-arriving changes in spelling included deleting *k* in many words ending in *ck* (as with *critic* rather than *critick*)—a preference that was seen before 1700 but took many years to become widespread.

In addition, the first great dictionaries of English did not appear until after 1700, and these would have at least some effect on spelling: John Kersey's *New English Dictionary* (1702), Nathaniel Bailey's *Universal Etymological English Dictionary*

(1721) and *Dictionarium Britannicum* (1730), and Samuel
Johnson's *Dictionary of the English Language* (1755). In general, however, British dictionaries mirrored the major
spellings already in use, rather than reforming the many
errant spellings of the language. At the most, the dictionaries would focus on listing major variant spellings or, at
times, would advocate one existing variant, rather than
offering sweeping reforms or new spellings. In the United
States, as I will discuss in Chapter 7, the situation was different. The former colony would be hungry for a dictionary that would help standardize American spellings, and
Noah Webster would help satisfy these lexical cravings.

Samuel Johnson, whose dictionary is now the best
known of the British dictionaries, seemed peeved that he
felt compelled to record, rather than reform, accepted
spellings. At first, he was explicit about wanting to "fix" the
language, but he appears to have learned such a task was
beyond even his skills or duties as a lexicographer. In his
preface, the great man wrote: "I have often been obliged to
sacrifice uniformity to custom; thus I write, in compliance
with a numberless majority, *convey* and *inveigh*, *deceit* and
receipt, *fancy* and *phantom*. . . ."

Dr. Johnson certainly was not shy about making his
opinions known elsewhere in his dictionary. For example,
he defines *oats* as a "grain, which in England is generally
given to horses, but in Scotland supports the people," while
excise is defined as a "hateful tax levied upon commodities,
and adjudged not by the common judges of property, but
wretches hired by those to whom excise is paid." Perhaps
his restraint in regard to spelling reflects what I mentioned
previously—the newfound respect people were giving to
Standard English spellings, even in cases where a standard
spelling seemed illogical.

Spoken English would continue to evolve, largely as a result of the development of dialects in America and other former colonies. Most English-speaking nations would eventually develop standards and spellings that differed in some regards from the London standard, yet all would be directly derived from the conventions established in Chancery halls of the fifteenth century.

These modifications notwithstanding, most linguists and historians agree that the major changes in English speech and, in particular, writing occurred by 1700. Middle English and certainly Old English might be difficult or impossible for people today to comprehend, but such is not the case with the English of 1700, especially in terms of spelling. Standard spelling, at long last, had arrived. The centuries of disinterest toward English standardization would be replaced by a single-minded expectation toward "correctness"—namely, that all educated English-speaking people must master these standard, yet often-illogical, spellings.

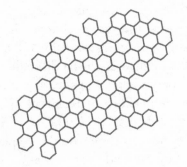

Can English Be Made to Behave?

o where does all this history take us?

While my intent has never been to offer just "how-to" advice, I confess that knowing the history of spelling will not necessarily improve a person's spelling ability. Many people, though, do improve their spelling once they find the subject interesting, and the history of spelling illustrates that the English system is not a mind-numbing, simplistic mechanism involving mere memorization. Rather, spelling is a tale of invading warriors and lost civilizations, of a people's resistance to becoming a nation, and of the rise of democracy and commerce in a land of monarchs and feudalism.

Sometimes, the greatest improvement in spelling occurs when a person feels more inclined to look closely at the spellings of words. I hope this brief history has encouraged readers to search spellings for their "hidden" aspects—such as etymology, embedded prejudices, and strange spellings that might have a logic behind them.

My historical overview should also have elucidated several major principles and assumptions about the status and future of spelling. In Chapter 4, I hinted at one key point when I claimed the history of spelling reveals why attempts to reform English spelling are doomed to fail, at least in regard to large-scale changes. Let me now be more explicit about this point, and then we will take a closer look at English-language spelling reforms around the globe—their possibilities, failures, successes, and results.

Language Change and Spelling Reform

No major reform of English spelling will make substantial gains, for spoken English will continue to change.

English spellings attempt to reflect pronunciation, so any true reform of spelling must be based on making the spelling of any given word have only one possible pronunciation. This is an extremely ambitious and problematic goal not only because there are notably different ways to pronounce words right now but because we have every reason to expect spoken English to continue to change.

A reformist must assume English will undergo no more changes, especially in terms of pronunciation. Yet we have already seen how susceptible English is to being altered. Most quirky spellings of today were once fine representations of how people pronounced the words, but the pronunciations have since changed, usually as a result of large-scale changes in speech. Many orthographic peculiarities, such as *knight*, came into being because their spelling was fixed at a point in history when the pronunciation had already changed, was in the process of changing, or would do so in the future. As mentioned earlier, virtually all silent consonants and most silent vowels of today were spoken at one time, including those in *knight*. We could transform this word to something like *nite*, though I am not sure how we will make it look different from *night* (also in need of reform). No matter how we change such spellings, we would have to assume their pronunciation is frozen.

Good luck. Nobody can stop English speech from changing; there are too many forces that promote increasing variation in written and spoken English. As the history of spelling shows, change can come from many sources, including immigrants, conquerors (no matter how invulnerable we think we are at present), technology (whether it be the printing press or the Internet), nationalism (as with the move to have red-blooded American spellings versus Britishisms), cultural or social movements (from the Renaissance to "geek speak" of today), and the borrowing of foreign words.

True, most linguistic historians agree English underwent relatively few large-scale changes in speech or orthography after 1700. Does this necessarily mean there will be no major changes in the future? My firm belief is we will see and hear such shifts by the middle of this century at the latest. Americans often assume their nation is converging in terms of dialect and pronunciation, moving toward some ubiquitous norm based on the way newscasters speak. This assumption is simply not true. Standard English does not automatically eliminate other varieties of English, and pronunciations are far from being frozen.

No doubt, certain aspects of regional or socioeconomic dialects are being lost, mainly in terms of word choice. It is difficult nowadays to find a Southerner who says "light bread" (young grocery clerks even in Alabama laugh at me for using the term to refer to "regular" bread, or they assume I want reduced-calorie bread). Nor is it easy to find a Midwesterner who uses "devil's darning needle" to refer to a dragonfly. Nonetheless, pronunciation differences exist in the United States and are increasing in many regards.

The leading authority on language variation in America is William Labov, professor of linguistics at the University of Pennsylvania. He points out that voice-recognition programs for computers and other technology must take into account the existence and growth of different ways to pronounce American English. Indeed, dialects of major cities such as New York, Detroit, Dallas, and Los Angeles differ more from one another now than they did in 1950. As one example, Labov has often pointed to the pronunciation of *cot* versus *caught*. Increasingly, Americans are pronouncing vowels of these words similarly; the two words are practically indistinguishable to many people. This merger of vowels is stronger in some regions (such as northeastern New England) and weaker in others (such as mid-Atlantic states). Not only do we have a language change in progress, but it is one that proceeds at a different pace across the nation. Such patterns will prevent, or at least forestall, the collapse of American dialects into one bland way of speaking.

Even though major changes in English pronunciation might not have occurred since 1700, the language has not been exactly stagnant either. Linguistic research reveals that, while older rural pronunciations might be fading away, new pronunciations are developing in urban areas. One source of change has been the influx of diverse foreign cultures into urban areas of America and England, along with the borrowing of words from an increasing array of languages. Keep in mind that loanwords often reflect the spelling systems of other languages. During the Renaissance, the English language borrowed hundreds of words from Latin, Greek, and French. But in more recent times, English has increased its sources for loanwords— for instance, by taking more words from Chinese, Spanish, and even aboriginal Australian (e.g., *boomerang*).

Given time, small-scale linguistic changes—such as those dealing with particular vowels and consonant combinations (as with *cot* and *caught*)—add up and create a lexical chain reaction. Language changes in some words influence changes in others having similar combinations of vowels, consonants, or sounds. The escalation has long been true in English, and it is not limited to speech changes. For instance, Middle English borrowed French words in which *ie* reflects the <e> sound, as in *grief*.

This spelling became more widespread than the traditional English *ee* (although *ee* survives in words such as *deed*). The French version became so popular it eventually caught on in numerous words—even words such as *belief* that date back to Old English and are not French at all. Such processes will continue to spread changes.

Highly populated areas are especially conducive to new ways to pronounce words. Changes in pronunciation are contagious. Urban areas, with their diverse mixing of cultures, can be enormous petri dishes in which new pronunciations are created and spread. In fact, linguists have given a name to one change that shows no signs of slowing down in America—the Northern Cities Shift, which is increasing the differences between Southern and Northern dialects. The most notable pronunciation shifts in North America involve vowels, but seeing as how all words have at least one vowel, these linguistic changes could greatly affect the pronunciation of many words, including terms that already seem in need of spelling reform.

Perhaps what we should really be wondering is why there have been so few major changes in English since the seventeenth century. Compared to the displacement of English after the Norman Conquest, the rise of the London dialect as a standard, and the Great Vowel Shift, the changes after 1700 have been relatively minor. Perhaps there is a tendency for scholars to claim English has not changed greatly, yet what might be closer to the truth is that *Standard* English—especially in England—has not changed much. Vernacular dialects of English in Great Britain and across the globe have changed over the years much more than Standard English.

I have to wonder as well if we have been undergoing a major linguistic shift but lack the perspective to realize it. Even with the comparatively abrupt beginning of Middle English, people in the eleventh century did not realize they were in the forefront of a vast linguistic movement, nor can you find the term

"Great Vowel Shift" in headlines of Elizabethan newspapers. When it comes to language, revolutions proceed incrementally and leisurely. Old words and pronunciations were never lined up to be beheaded; rather, they were gradually retired or converted into the rank and file of a new lexicon. Possibly, our grandchildren will one day ask us what it was like in the days when people made the <r> sound in *here*. Our descendants will surely snicker at the way we use "Modern English," as if our language of today will always be considered modern. Maybe there will be a Postmodern English period, though I fear academics have so robbed "postmodern" of any meaning that it will never recover.

One could argue that we should forget about dialects and simply base our reformed spellings on Standard English pronunciations, or at least those given in reputable dictionaries. Let's pretend that the best dictionaries agree on these pronunciations (they do not). If the goal is for spellings to mirror the way we speak, then keep in mind relatively few people speak in Standard English. Take the United States, for example. Standard English is not a native dialect for any particular regional, social-economic, or ethnic group of Americans. It is a variety of English we learn, primarily in school. For most of us who gain competency with Standard English, it never completely replaces our dialect or daily ways of speaking. Instead, Standard English is a style we mainly use in formal situations, written and spoken.

Yes, learning Standard English can cause a person to use or avoid certain linguistic features even in casual discourse. This person might, for instance, almost entirely stop using double negatives. However, few people adopt Standard English as their sole basis for communicating, especially in terms of pronunciation.

In other words, if the goal of spelling reform is to replace our system with one that better reflects how we really talk, then the new spellings should not be based merely on Standard English pronunciations, even if we decide what these are. Such pronunciations do not accurately reflect the varieties of spoken English within one country, much less English around the world. History shows that pronunciations will change, and English is not like a computer program that can be updated as needed. I for one do not foresee Modern English 1.03b in our future discussions of the language.

Three Alphabetic Problems

The messy history of linguistic changes, the influx of various languages, and the ongoing shifts in power in English-speaking countries have resulted in letter/sound configurations that create some unusual sentences. For several years now, people have been e-mailing lists of bewildering sentences such as these to illustrate how illogical our spellings are:

- I did not object to the object.
- A seamstress and a sewer fell down into a sewer line.
- The soldier decided to desert his dessert in the desert.
- A bass was painted on the head of the bass drum.
- The wind was too strong to wind the sail.
- Because there is no time like the present, he thought it was time to present the present.

The history of spelling explains how such spellings and pronunciations can exist in English. English has several heteronyms (sometimes called *homographs*); these are words spelled identically but having different meanings and pronunciations. In a nutshell, English contains many heteronyms because conventions for spelling and pronunciation were not evenly applied as various words from different languages were standardized.

For instance, both uses of *object* in the first example above came into English at the same time (around 1400) and derive from the same Latin term, yet pronunciation changes in America as well as England would not affect the two words in the same way, probably because these changes tend to affect the most common words first.

Other heteronyms have a more complex history, as seen in the second example. The word *sewer* in the sense of one who sews goes back to Old English *siwian* or *seowian*. In contrast, *sewer* in terms of a nasty stretch of water arrived later in Middle English from the French word *sewiere* or *essewer*. This French term, because of both the official status of French and the government's interest in sewers, was soon regularized as *sewer*. However, the more rustic Old English term took centuries to be standardized into *sewer* (one who sews). As late as the 1600s, *sew* rhymed with *new*. Even in 1800, *sews* was often spelled *sowes*. Perhaps, then, the spelling changed to make *sow* and *sew* dissimilar. Another factor in the development of *sewer* might involve the "three-letter rule," which I will describe in Chapter 10. Essentially, spelling *sew* as *so* was never really an option because English avoids words with two letters unless they do not by themselves have much meaning (as with *so*).

Ultimately, the source of problematic spellings such as the two meanings and pronunciations of *sewer* involves the unhurried standardization of English—and the lack of an authoritative entity that would eliminate such orthographic inconsistencies.

In the previous chapters, I described in detail how many English sounds and letters have changed. These changes—such as the loss of the <b> sound in words such as *comb*—help explain why many words have a spelling that seems inconsistent or no longer phonetic. I have not covered *all* of the linguistic changes that have affected today's spellings. To describe every odd spelling or historical influence would be excessive.

There are a few larger conclusions we can make based just on what I have covered so far.

Mark Twain once said the problem with our alphabet is that it "doesn't know how to spell, and can't be taught." To be a tad more specific, the history of spelling reveals at least three flaws of our alphabetic system and why it fails to match spoken English.

1. At Least Fourteen Sounds in English Have No Corresponding Letter

Even though few if any languages using a phonetic system can really meet the ideal goal of having one letter reserved exclusively for each distinct and meaningful sound in a given language, English orthography has a number of omissions for a language that is purportedly phonetic. Among the most notable oversights are the following:

voiced	\<th\>	(*there*)
unvoiced	\<th\>	(*both*)
	\<sh\>	(*shoot*)
	\<ch\>	(*chop*)
	\<aw\>	(*sought*)
	\<oi\>	(*boy*)

Many of us were taught that each of these sounds, such as what I have fairly arbitrarily referred to as \<oi\>, is really two different sounds. Our spellings reaffirm this mistaken assumption, for one way we deal with the missing sounds is to represent them by using two letters to stand for one sound. Nevertheless, the \<oi\> sound is *one* sound. The letters *o*, *i*, and *y* are marginally related, if at all, to the sound we make in words such as *boy*. Try saying any possible pronunciation of *o* and *y* separately, and you will confirm that no combination adds up to <oi>. The two sounds of *th* might be the most obvious examples of bogus stand-ins. The letters *t* and *h* do not culminate in the sounds they make when written together.

2. Many Letters Duplicate Each Other

This problem is twofold. First, a few letters are truly unnecessary. The sound we hear when the letter *q* is pronounced is actually *two* distinct sounds: <k> and <w>. Anything *c* can do by itself—not counting *ch*—can be done by *s* or *k*. And *x* can be replaced by *ks* (*box*), *gs* (*exist*), or even *z* (*xylophone*).

Second, many letters duplicate not only the sounds made by *q*, *c*, and *x* but those made by the rest of the alphabet. Today, we have few letters that stand for just one sound apiece. It is a wonder there is not an identity crisis among members of the alphabet. The source of the problem is largely a result of borrowing words from languages in which letters stand for different sounds than what they traditionally stood for in English. The letters *f*, *m*, *v*, and *z* almost never switch-hit, but they are the exceptions. As discussed earlier, the sound made by *c* might seem hard to anticipate. According to Richard Venezky's study, *c* stands for <k> about 74 percent of the time, but a notable 22 percent of its appearances involve the <s> sound. The letter *g* can be <g> as in *great* or <j> as in *heritage*. Vowels such as *a* can be long (*bake*) or short (*bad*), yet each vowel can help create other sounds as well (*bar*).

It is bad enough that almost any single letter can stand for more than one sound, but equally confounding is the fact that some letters pair up to duplicate existing sounds. As mentioned previously, sometimes it is good when letters pair up—albeit arbitrarily—so they can represent sounds that no one letter can handle. For example, *ch* allows us to represent the <ch> sound in *chop*.

Nevertheless, sometimes letters gang up to produce a sound already handled by one letter. The letter *u* is perfectly able to reflect the vowel heard in *rule*. That does not keep *oo* from making the same sound in *tool*. The same applies to *ew* in *jewel*, as well as *ou* in *through*. These combinations, all derived from pronunciation shifts and loanwords, needlessly duplicate what *u* all by itself could do.

3. Some Letters Are Silent

As I will mention later, this third problem is most detrimental in terms of silent consonants, rather than vowels. The following are just a few examples:

g̲nome

sw̲ord

cast̲le

autumn̲

sig̲n

althoug̲h̲

bac̲k

list̲en

w̲rite

Usually, the source of this problem goes back to changes that occurred after a spelling was set. In this way, *k* became fossilized in *knife* even though long ago people stopped pronouncing what was essentially a <k> sound in that word.

English words contain more silent letters than we might realize if we consider the way people really speak. In various places around the world as diverse as Australia, Boston, South Carolina, and London, the <r> sound after vowels (known as "postvocalic *r*") is not pronounced. You can "hear" this silent phenomenon in the way some people pronounce words such as *car*, *here*, and *Harvard*. Depending on who is speaking and to whom, a listener might consider the postvocalic *r* to be quaint, prestigious, nonstandard, or backward, but *r* is indeed silent for many English-speaking people of all socioeconomic classes and educational levels. These deletions do not appear to be creating a surplus of *r*'s. In dialects such as Southern Appalachian, speakers often add <r> after vowels, as in <yeller> for <yellow>.

How Horrid Is English Spelling Anyway?

These three problems account for most words having spellings that do not reflect how the words are pronounced. Some terms are difficult to peg down in terms of which shortcoming(s) they have. The word *colonel* is a notorious example. It has letters that duplicate other letters (*c* is used for the <k> sound). It also seems the combination *olo* is standing for <er>, while *e* is making either the short <u> or <e> sound depending on one's pronunciation. You could even claim one letter or another is silent rather than working with others to produce the <er> sound. Historically, this irritating spelling goes back to how two forms of the same word were borrowed in the 1500s. Around 1550, English took the term *coronel* from French, but a few decades later *colonel* was introduced, probably because this spelling better reflected an Italian pedigree. Ultimately, English kept the older pronunciation but adapted the Italian-based spelling.

But how many *colonels*, *knights*, and *gnomes* do we have in English? Spelling reformists have always pointed to such words yet rarely admit these are the exceptions. Most words in English bear reasonable resemblance to common pronunciations.

We also need to consider *how* people read. True, we read more easily when there is a phonetic relationship between each letter and each sound we would make when saying the word aloud, but adults in particular do not read by painstakingly stumbling through each letter in a book or newspaper article. We see the entire word in the context of what we have already read and then make sense of the term. The importance in terms of spelling is simple: it is a mistake to assume spelling must be 100 percent phonetic. Having a perfect "one-letter, one-sound" system is unnecessary because we do not read merely by looking at each letter and translating it into a sound. Although part of the reading process involves individual letters and their relationship to speech, primarily we read (and spell) by examining the larger context of the word and the entire sentence—a fact recognized by all credible reading researchers whether they subscribe to whole-language or phonics-based instruction. In fact, this way of reading and learning to spell does not have to be explicitly taught. In any language, people naturally acquire a subconscious understanding of what sorts of sound and letter combinations are possible, common, and rare.

In a study published in 2002, Rebecca Treiman of Washington University and her colleagues at Wayne State University examined how college students attempted to spell made-up words. Now, before you assume that encouraging students to spell nonsense words is one reason Americans do not spell well, consider what the researchers found in terms of the students' spelling and reading strategies.

In the experiment, students would hear nonsense words such as <glite> and <glibe> and then offer a spelling. With this pair of words, they would frequently use the letters *-igh* to make the long <i> in <glite>. Rarely did any of the subjects use these letters when spelling <glibe>. What this research shows is that people spell by considering the entire context of a word and by drawing on what they have internalized about English spelling in general. For instance, *igh* creates the <i> sound when followed by <t>. The words *sight*, *might*, and *fight* are common examples. The students, although they were not always totally aware of why they made their choices, would draw on their internalized knowledge of written English and spell <glite> as *glight*. No word in English uses *ighb* to make the long <i>, so students rarely spelled <glibe> as *glighb*. Readers, then, take into account not just the individual letter or sound when spelling and reading. They look at the larger environment.

For many people, *ghoti* is the poster child for spelling reform. Usually attributed to playwright George Bernard Shaw, this odd spelling supposedly reflects how *fish* could be spelled based on other English terms. This deliberate misspelling—the most famous example of the alleged failure of English orthography—overlooks the fact that spelling deals with the *whole* word, not just particular letters and sounds. In addition to pointing out the inadequacies of capitalism and colonialism, Shaw wanted to reform English spelling, and the story goes that he claimed *fish* could be spelled *ghoti* according to letter/sound relationships found in elsewhere in English. The <f> in *fish* could be made by *gh* (as in *cough*). The short <i> could be made by *o* (as in *women*). And the <sh> we hear in *fish* could be made by *ti* (as in *nation*).

Two problems taint this example. First, Shaw probably did not really come up with it; a colleague relayed it to Shaw, who apparently knew this was not a good example of the limitations of our spelling system. Second, *ghoti* fails to take into account that choosing the correct letters to spell a word depends, as Shaw undoubtedly knew, on the rest of the word. There are reasons why people never misspell *fish* as *ghoti* unless they are spelling reformists.

First off, the letters *gh* make an <f> sound only toward the end of a word, as with *tough* and *laugh*. Even then, certain vowels must precede *gh* (note how *thigh* is not pronounced <thif>). The <i> sound heard in *women* is unique. This plural form kept its Old English pronunciation even though *woman* changed to its current pronunciation during Middle English. Finally, *ti* never makes the <sh> sound unless combined with *o* and *n* to create *-tion* (as in *sta<u>tion</u>*).

The <sh> sound is another example used to illustrate the shortcomings of English spelling. The authors of *1001 Commonly Misspelled Words* point out there are at least seventeen ways in English to represent this sound, as seen in these examples:

admi<u>ss</u>ion	ini<u>ti</u>ate	pre<u>ss</u>ure
appre<u>ci</u>ate	lu<u>x</u>ury	<u>sch</u>ist
atten<u>ti</u>on	nau<u>se</u>a	<u>sh</u>ock
con<u>sci</u>ous	ma<u>ch</u>ine	stan<u>chi</u>on
exten<u>si</u>on	musta<u>che</u>	<u>s</u>ure
fu<u>ch</u>sia	o<u>ce</u>an	

The <sh> sound can certainly take these forms, but once again, whether a letter such as *t* can stand for <sh> depends on the immediate lexical environment, on where *t* appears in the word in relation to other letters. For instance, *t* will never be <sh> at the beginning of a word.

I need not labor through each of these seventeen variants to make my point. You do not need a linguist or a grammarian to realize you use letters such as *si* to make <sh> only in certain words or situations. These constraints on <sh> and other letter/sound relationships are acquired naturally. Teaching such lists of all possibilities would, of course, do nothing more than confuse anyone attempting to learn written English. The "*i* before *e*" rule might be the only spelling rule most of us remember, but that does not mean there aren't other rules our brains have assimilated.

But the biggest flaw in concluding English is chaotic based on lists such as the example is this: you would have to assume all variations are equally possible. There really is not a mere one in seventeen chance the <sh> sound will be made by *sh*. Most words having the <sh> sound use *sh*, with some variants (especially *che*, *chs*, and *se*) being exceedingly rare. While we cannot deny written English has many ways to represent each meaningful sound, that fact does not open the floodgates of chaos. The options for spelling any given word are significantly decreased because of predictable patterns—patterns which limit our choice of letters depending on where they would appear in the word.

Still, we could reduce the options further. People could learn to spell *ocean* as *ashun*, or *machine* as *masheen*. We would face, however, the greatest barrier to spelling reform in any language: once people appreciate the notion of having consistent spellings, they are extremely reluctant to change any spelling with which they have become familiar, even in cases of illogical spellings. Stubbornness? Perhaps, but this reaction is the flip side of the desire to have constancy in spelling.

Standardization is possible only when people appreciate the value of spelling words consistently, but this larger desire for regularity means people also want to keep individual words the way they are. We cannot have one attitude without the other.

It's Not Easy Being *E*

Another favorite target of spelling reformists is the abundance of silent letters in our English vocabulary. For me, the most annoying silent letters are consonants that hang around long after most people stopped pronouncing them, as with *r* in *February*, or the notoriously mute *k* and *gh* in *knight*. To be silent, as my spouse reminds me occasionally, is not always a bad idea. We need to recall that silent letters often have a purpose—or even an unintended but useful side effect. Nobody planned it this way, but *k* and *gh* distinguish *knight* from the homonym *night*, just as silent letters help differentiate *sight* from *site* and *cite*.

The most common and important silent letter has to be the much-maligned *e*, long condemned by many reformists (such as Noah Webster) even though some concede its value. I want to give silent *e* special attention because it is a reflection of our entire system—flawed at times, yet more logical than we tend to think. Silent *e* is so much a part of English orthography that we tend to silence *e* even when we should not. Americans tend to pronounce the German brand name (not to mention family name) *Porsche* as <porsh> even though the *e* should be pronounced, albeit as <uh> rather than short or long <e>. As I'm sure some Porsche owners would love to remind us, the error is almost as bad as removing the <uh> sound in *Toyota*.

Silent *e* plays a crucial role in English spelling and is not something to be surrendered easily. Almost any letter can make more than one sound, but like *Roberts' Rules of Order*, silent *e* restores order and prevents needless squabbling among letters by indicating who speaks and in what manner.

As we learned in elementary school, silent *e* at the end of a word alerts us the preceding vowel will be "long" (or as students like to say, the silent *e* makes the vowel "say its name"). More specifically, the pattern is as follows:

vowel + consonant + silent e = long vowel pronunciation.

Thus, the pronunciation <bar> becomes <bare> when *e* is added, while <nod> becomes <node>. Sure, other devices could be used to tell us how to pronounce the vowel in words such as *mine* and *isotope*, but silent *e* works just about as well as any other choice. For English spelling to be truly phonetic, we should invent new letters for our alphabet so short and long vowels would look completely different. Even most spelling reformers balk at cranking out new letters, although from time to time a few extremists suggest we simply need to start pronouncing silent letters to fix the problem.

Admittedly, the silent *e* pattern noted here works most of the time, but it is much more complex and perhaps more problematic than what we have been taught.

The problem is not that there are other ways to create a long vowel, as in *meet* or *meat*. We could even overlook the long-vowel words that end in -*ld* yet lack a silent *e*, as in *mild* and *told*. On the surface, the greater problem appears to be that many words ending in silent *e* do *not* follow the "long vowel" pattern. However, this does mean the silent *e* is useless in such instances. We just need to be aware of its multiple functions. Here are a few examples in which *e* does something besides—or in addition to—showing a vowel is long:

have	sparse
love	nurse
glove	lapse
mediate	house
morale	dense
mice	terse
trace	bronze
stage	mustache
age	awe
image	belle
range	roe

Technically, silent *e* has at least a dozen different functions, although a few are uncommon. In some instances, *e* is added to distinguish a word from a homophone (*bell* vs. *belle*) or near-homophone (*moral* vs. *morale*). Almost always, though, *e* indicates how to pronounce at least one previous letter (more evidence that readers see the whole word rather than proceeding letter by letter). The vast majority of silent consonants we have today were once pronounced, but silent vowels have long been used to show how to pronounce a word. The letter *e* was sometimes quiet in Middle English, but it was frequently used also to represent the schwa (or <uh>) sound we are supposed to hear in *Porsche*.

Silent *e* today can indicate that more than just one preceding vowel should be pronounced in a long fashion, as in *mediate*. At other times, *e* tells us how to pronounce consonants. For example, it indicates the *s* in *nurse* is not pronounced with the voiced <z> we hear in *Mars* or *jars*.

Silent *e* is especially useful when showing how to pronounce consonants while also avoiding ending a word with letters that bother our orthographic sensibilities. The hard <g> sound in *stag*, for instance, becomes <j> in *stage* because of *e*, which also makes *a* become a long vowel. English disdains ending words with some letters, and *j* might be the least favorite ending of all, being limited to a handful of loanwords such as Hindi *raj* and Muslim *taj*. For unknown reasons, it is not so much a final <j> sound that English avoids, just the letter *j* itself. In terms such as *stage* and *age*, silent *e* indicates *g* makes the <j> sound so we can avoid this unusual pet peeve against a final *j*.

English also avoids ending a letter with a single *s*. This tendency is not arbitrary. In general, a single *s* at the end of word is reserved for showing possession (*Ted's*), plurality (*boys*), or verbs used with third-person subjects (*hates*, as in "It hates me"). To avoid confusion with these grammatical structures, silent *e* is added to avoid final *s* in words such as *lapse* and *house*. (By the way, a double-*s* ending is permissible, as in *mess*, but doubling tends to be used only when certain vowels are used.)

In a similar vein, one function of *e* at the end of *mice* and *trace* is to help us know what sound *c* makes: it makes an <s> sound, not the <k> we hear in *magic* and *static*. You would think the letter *k* could be used in these last two examples, giving us *magik* and *statik*. But again for reasons not entirely clear, English has a bias about letters that can end a word—this time, a bias against a vowel followed by *k*. Each language has its own particular preferences and prejudices. Many languages embrace the option of ending letters with a vowel plus *k*, but English happens not to be one. The *-ck* ending is certainly acceptable, as in *click*, but *k* alone is rare. The exceptions tend to be slang words such as *boychik* or, more commonly, loan-words such as African *trek*, Russian *Bolshevik*, and Inuit *anorak* (originally a type of jacket, but also British slang for *nerd* or for a person who is too excited about watching trains).

People complain that English spelling is inconsistent, yet perhaps they do not look in the right places. English is highly consistent about avoiding spellings that end in *j* or a vowel plus *k*, not to mention a few other regular biases that reduce the number of possible spellings a word might have. Silent *e* helps maintain this consistency by letting us know to pronounce <j> and <k> sounds in spite of the absence of *j* and *k* letters.

Sometimes, the purposes of silent *e* are difficult to determine and arise from old concerns now forgotten. Middle English printers frequently added *e* merely to make words longer in an effort to create a justified right margin, but that does not seem to have had a permanent effect on any spelling involving silent *e*. Consider, however, the interesting spellings of *love* and *give*. Silent *e* seems unnecessary because the vowels are short. The simple way to explain away *e* in such words is to point out English also avoids ending a word with *v*. The real reasons are more complex, involving scribes and printers once again, as well as a monk.

According to one theory, the visual appearance of another letter—*w*—is part of the reason we have silent *e* in "*v* words" such as *love*, but first we need to return to early Middle English. Beginning about this time, an increasingly popular way to indicate a vowel was short rather than long was to double the next consonant. We can mainly thank a monk named Orm from about the year 1200 for this strategy. In a lifeless poem of some ten thousand lines (which he named *The Ormulum* in his honor),

Orm doubled consonants to provide a much-needed regular method for identifying short vowels. His strategy survives in a great many short words of today, including *spell*, *stiff*, and *moss*. A similar pattern exists with words of more than one syllable such as *happy* and *hopping* (the doubling also distinguishes the latter from *hoping*). Later in Middle English, vowels would also be doubled to show they were long (as in *deed*).

In the 1580s, Richard Mulcaster's *Elementarie*—the first substantive text attempting to provide written rules for English spelling—tried to standardize English spelling in other ways, but, as often happens, the reforms were only partially successful and ultimately led to more inconsistency. Schoolmaster Mulcaster had no problem with *e*, describing it as "a letter of marvelous use in the writing of our tongue . . . even where it seemeth idle." He actually encouraged silent *e* to indicate long vowels; his bigger concern was excess letters. Mulcaster hoped to deplete English of the double-consonant pattern in particular (he was not fond of double vowels either). As one of the more successful spelling reformists in English, he helped words like *putt* and *bedd* simplify into *put* and *bed*. Obviously, people were reluctant to give up Orm's double consonants, so doubling continued despite Mulcaster's success with some spellings. Perhaps thinking compromise was most practical, even Mulcaster was not consistent in his reforms. He tolerated doubled letters in the middle of words to separate syllables as well as certain doubled consonants at the end of words, such as *ll* in *tall*.

Words such as *love* and *give* were, unfortunately, not among the words that opted for Mulcaster's simplification. Otherwise, we would have *lov* and *giv* along with *put* and *bed*. People felt many words should include a signpost indicating vowels are short, yet the old method of doubling consonants did not work for words that would end in a double *v*. English avoids ending words with *v* because doubling the letter would, at least to early scribes and printers, look too much like *w*. Thus, *e* seems to have been added to most "*v* words" having a short vowel, rather than using the more common strategy of doubling consonants to show the vowel is short. The strategy was undoubtedly a poor choice because *e* is primarily used to indicate *long* vowels. Why this fault was disregarded is a mystery despite the fact that Mulcaster clearly considered this unusual orthography when laying out his rules.

Silent *e*, in brief, usually has a purpose—several in fact. Though sometimes held up as evidence that we need a spelling revolution, only in oddities such as *love* is the silent *e* truly superfluous, and even these anomalies have regularity about them (such as how silent *e* is used to avoid what would otherwise be a word ending in *v*).

Despite the three flaws I listed earlier in this chapter, English orthography is not as horrid as some people would have us believe. As I have discussed at length, the dynamic history of England resulted in a system of spelling that is far from perfect and has many eccentricities, such as an ample supply of silent consonants.

But neither is the system chaotic. English spelling rests somewhere between perfection and chaos, yet large-scale reforms would not solve what is typically seen as the fundamental problem: namely, that English spelling and speech do not always match.

If Finland Can, Why Can't We?

ome countries have undergone spelling and language reforms, but English-spelling reformists neglect to mention that most were far from successful. Nor are they necessarily feasible given the nature of English and English-speaking nations.

French and German Reforms

Reforms depend on some type of regulatory organization or an authority that can dictate or recommend (with considerable clout) linguistic changes. The best-known example is supposedly the French Academy (*L'Académie française*), established in the 1630s in Paris. This group certainly seems impressive enough to institute changes; its forty members are referred to as "the immortals" and have included notables such as Louis Pasteur, Victor Hugo, and Voltaire. They even wear special feathered hats and—unless they are females or members of the clergy—are given ceremonial swords (just in case the pen is not mightier than the sword after all). Despite these trimmings, the Academy merely recommends changes or gives its bless-ings on matters related to the French language.

In fact, the conservative views of these immortals often clash with the socialist or liberal inclinations of the French gov-ernment and populace. When the government considered giv-ing official recognition to various regional languages and dialects in France, one member of the Academy, Jean-Marie Rouart, responded: "At the very moment that our language is being bastardized by Anglo-Saxon expressions, it is to be undermined from within by having to compete with local dialects." A French publication in favor of reforms in French spelling proudly has as its motto, "Not a single useless letter," yet the Academy frequently opposes the journal and proceeds with its own conservative approach to reforming French spelling.

When the French government and Academy do agree, the results are often inconsequential. Perhaps the Academy's lead-ing concern, and failure, is capping the flow of English spellings and words into the everyday vocabulary of French citizens, who for some reason prefer "air bag" to "*coussin gon-fable de protection.*" In 2005, Microsoft finally added an option allowing users to spell-check their French by using what is described as being the Academy's preferences, rather than the traditional spellings. Perhaps Microsoft's implicit support will prove sufficient to boost the Academy's influence.

Those who argue in favor of reforming English point out what they deem successful reforms of other languages, and the June 1990 reform of French spelling is usually given as an example. The Academy is often credited with this attempt, but it was actually the result of a special governmental body, *Con-seil supérieur de la langue française*. The French Academy initially endorsed this 1990 spelling reform, but members soon found they were in disagreement with one another as well as with the *Conseil*. The Academy almost completely withdrew its support in 1991, although Microsoft seems unaware of this fact. Throughout France, few of the proposed spellings have supplanted the traditional spellings, even though the changes called for were relatively modest.

Similar results occurred with German reforms of the 1990s. German spelling and its letter/sound relationships are more consistent than some languages, but it is certainly not immune to problems. Most of the latest proposed spellings reflect an attempt to make the spellings look more German. One of the few English loanwords to be rehabilitated was *ketchup*, which was modified to *ketschup*. Actually, English borrowed the word from Malaysia around 1700 but changed the spelling along with the recipe, which originally included fish brine.

The German reform was not ambitious. Even after the reforms, the German word for *fox* could be spelled in more than sixty ways. The reforms were still widely opposed. By law, the spellings that were approved must now be taught in German schools, yet many Germans—along with several newspapers and magazines—continue to use older spellings anyway. As often happens with spelling reforms, the German reforms have so far done little more than increase the number of ways words can be spelled.

Spelling reformists regularly present lists of countries where spelling reforms supposedly took place, but attempting a reform does not mean it succeeds. If individuals are reluctant to change spellings, nations are even more stubborn. Sometimes, even changing the spelling of a few words can seem to threaten a nation's identity. In 2004, Latvia—home to one of the world's most consistent spelling systems—joined the European Union but strongly opposed the rule that all members use the spelling *euro* when referring to the common currency. The Latvian spelling is only slightly different: *eiro*. The nation's foreign minister said, "It's a political question although we're not trying to show anyone how strong we are." Somehow, the matter sounds as though it concerns both politics and the strength of a nation's will against linguistic conformity. The debates continue as other nations balk at this orthographic oppression.

The Case of Finland

The example of success almost always brought up by spelling reformers involves Finnish orthography. This is indeed one instance when large-scale spelling reforms achieved notable success by regularizing an entire spelling system. Along with Spanish, Hungarian, and the Korean orthography known as Hangul, Finnish is among the most logical phonemic alphabets ever known. Almost always, a given Finnish letter will stand for only one Finnish sound. While Finnish words can be unusually lengthy, each is spelled just as it sounds. Finnish spelling was reformed and stabilized after careful planning and implementation, and few can deny this success in Finland.

Keep in mind the obvious: English is not Finnish. Spelling aside, there are notable differences between these two languages and cultures. Although Swedish is used by a small percentage of the population, Finland is home to only two major dialects, as compared to at least a dozen major dialects of English in just the United States.

In Finnish, whether or not a particular vowel can appear in a word depends on what other vowel is used in the same word. The vowel *y*, for instance, will not be used if *u*, *o*, or *a* is used elsewhere in a word. English disdains such segregation. English and Finnish do not always employ the same sounds either. Finnish has fewer sounds than most languages, making it less complicated to match letters with sounds. While Finnish has eight vowels, it has only thirteen consonants. In Finnish, for instance, you do not hear the "voiced" letters *b* and *g*, unless they are taken from English loanwords, which are steadily encroaching onto Finnish lands. (Nokia Corporation, Finland's best-known business, now uses English as its language of choice, and English is easily the first choice of Finnish students learning a foreign language, as is the case in many countries.)

In regard to spelling reforms, the greatest difference between the two languages is that there is a particular variety of Finnish devoted to formal communication, especially writing. Certainly, English has what is often called Standard English, which varies from nation to nation but as a whole offers a basis for formal discourse. Standard English, though, pales in comparison to the Finnish equivalent. Standard English is certainly taught in schools and used in formal writing, but English-speaking people normally do not recognize it as being a markedly different variety of English. We tend to think of Standard English as merely the correct way of writing and speaking. Most Americans are not even familiar with the term "Standard English." In Finland, the language used in formal situations has a stronger identity, even having its own name to distinguish it from casual Finnish. The distinctness of the two Finnish varieties makes spelling reforms much easier to develop and accept.

Practically all Finnish people use both the formal and informal varieties of their language: *puhekieli* and *yleiskieli*. The word *puhekieli* means "spoken language" and is the colloquial Finnish used in everyday speech. Seldom is *puhekieli* used in any writing except in informal contexts, such as blogs on the Internet.

In contrast, *yleiskieli* is the formal Finnish taught in schools and used in newscasts, churches, speeches, and other situations in which everyday Finnish would be considered too casual. Unlike the everyday variety of Finnish, *yleiskieli* is not a first language for Finns, nor is it identified today with either of the major Finnish dialects.

These two varieties differ greatly in terms of grammar and vocabulary. For instance, "my book" in formal *yleiskieli* is "*minum kirjani*," while "*mun kirja*" is the same phrase in *puhekieli*.

The Finns even have a name for the written counterpart of the formal variety of speech: *kirjakieli*, which literally means "book language." This written version was developed relatively late in Finnish history and stems from the work of Bishop Mikael Agricola, who in the midsixteenth century composed the first major texts in Finnish. Until that time, most writing in Finland was in German, Latin, or Swedish (the latter was the official language of Finland and heavily influenced *kirjakieli*). This written form of Finnish is usually even more formal than its oral counterpart, *yleiskieli*. In fact, the written variety is more complex and not as conducive to conciseness, making it less suitable for speech.

By setting aside a form of Finnish intended exclusively for formal writing, the Finns sidestepped the problem of language change, dialects, and people's reluctance to change the way they speak. Having originated in an era when many Finns did not read or write (especially in Finnish), *kirjakieli* is now an accepted part of the Finnish life. Most important, *kirjakieli* was carefully planned and designed to be almost completely phonetic. When compared to the relationship between *kirjakieli* and casual Finnish, Standard English and casual English are extremely similar. Reforming Standard English spellings along the lines of the Finnish reform would mean setting up an entirely new "book language" for English. Such an extensive revision of our language is clearly impractical.

Many Americans will boast that we can do anything the Finns can do except play their brand of baseball, which involves a pitcher standing almost within arm's length of the batter. We should not view spelling reform as a matter of national pride and honor. We must take into consideration how profoundly different our languages are.

Realistically, English-speaking people have no chance at this point in our linguistic and social histories of developing and implementing a written variety of English that would be distinct from any one dialect or way of speaking. Perhaps if the British had latched upon this notion when written English was being reinvented, as in the sixteenth century, they could have created a spelling system based on clear logic and greater consistency. But nobody seized the day, and we now must work with our present system, with spelling reforms coming slowly in the form of an occasional word being simplified here and there.

When Reforms Succeed

Timing is everything. Major reforms that have been successfully implemented have at least one of three characteristics.

First, successful reforms are more likely when literacy is not widespread, making it easier to change a system simply because fewer people are involved or have investment in maintaining the status quo of spellings. The beginnings of the Finnish reforms, for example, took place when Finnish was not even the nation's official language, written or spoken. Few sixteenth-century Finns took it personally when Mikael Agricola and his reformist successors began creating a formal variety of written Finnish. In English, the language reforms that were more or less organized tended to occur when most people were illiterate—such as when Wessex became the standard in late Old English and in the fifteenth century when Chancery scribes created a standard based on a London dialect.

Earlier, I alluded to the second ingredient for a large-scale language reform: someone with authority or considerable influence has to be involved in implementing the changes. This "someone" does not have to be a particular person, but the larger the group becomes, the less likely the reform will succeed. Committees tend to spend most of their time disagreeing with one another or developing safe but ineffectual compromises, as with the French Academy. In fact, language reforms usually are most successful when this authority figure is closely linked, as often happens, to a third characteristic: larger cultural or political transformations.

Take, for example, the unparalleled success of Turkish language reform. Termed *dil devrimi*, the reform was led by former military leader Mustafa Kemal Atatürk in the late 1920s. Atatürk also happened to be the founder of the Turkish Republic and its influential first president (with dictatorial powers), a position he held for fifteen years. Recognizing the need to bring Turkey into the twentieth century through education and global influence, he demanded Turks replace their thousand-year-old Arabic script with the Latin alphabet. The story goes that his experts told him it would take five years or more, and Atatürk replied, "We shall do it within five months." Literally overnight in some instances, Arabic script disappeared from public places.

Children and adults were required to learn the new alphabet, and literacy dramatically increased. Portable chalkboard in hand, the president himself would teach the new alphabet in schools and along public streets. In one of the quickest yet most successful reforms of language in history, this charismatic and powerful leader succeeded where Turkish intellectuals and less-powerful nationalists of the previous century had failed. The success of this standardization of a Turkish language, both written and spoken, is especially amazing considering the diverse dialects, languages, and ethnic groups that existed in Turkey. Atatürk's language reforms were part of a much larger cultural revolution he led, one that included secular reform and women's rights.

What happened in Turkey was not just a spelling reform but a language revolution. Despite the many economic and political benefits, the drawbacks are worth mentioning. The linguistic changes were so great that relatively few Turks today can read most of the Turkish and Ottoman writing produced before the twentieth century, although some translations are available. In an effort to rid Turkish of "foreign" words, many useful words, especially those from Arabic and Persian, were discarded and never truly replaced. The rhetoric of allowing only "pure Turkish" words was often carried to such an extreme that it smacks of bigotry. Making it illegal to use the Arabic alphabet was effective but infringes on civil rights (as some British citizens similarly argue when laws force them to use the metric system of weights and measures). The debates continue to ebb and flow in Turkey regarding whether the language reforms themselves need to be reformed in favor of either more traditional or more modern styles.

Although not nearly as successful in terms of creating a clear and consistent spelling system, the German reform of 1902 also came at the right time and had the "lead players" who had the clout to put the somewhat-flawed reforms into effect. The German Empire was still new at this time, having been created in 1871 by consolidating a loose confederacy of Germanic states into a unified power having both a parliament and a monarchy. The Germanic culture, though ages old, had been only recently reborn into a nation when its legislature approved substantial revisions of its spelling in 1902. Perhaps not surprisingly, the German reforms amounted to scores of rules attempting to cover almost every orthographic possibility, creating considerable confusion.

The German government was one authoritative force that helped these rules go into effect, but equally influential was the dictionary of Konrad Duden, which was largely the basis of the reforms. Two decades earlier, his grand dictionary had appeared with no real competition in the new empire, and Germans quickly followed his orthographic lead. In fact, the Duden dictionaries would set the standard after both the Second and Third Reichs were buried in ashes. This dictionary's clout remained solid until the 1950s, when competition increased along with discontent regarding the 1902 reforms.

In other languages, spelling and language reforms, even when imperfect, tend to need a powerful promoter who can implement the new systems, either with public support or by sheer force. These reforms also tend to require a special timing in a nation's history, occurring when the society is at the threshold of major cultural changes.

Consider these additional examples. First, in the late 1800s, Latvians took new pride in their language, which had long been treated as a peasant language by influential German nobles throughout the region, and in 1908 a major and highly successful spelling reform took place at the same time Latvians were moving toward becoming an independent nation, which occurred in 1918. Second, the adoption of Castilian as standard Spanish can be traced back to King Alfonso the Learned, whose thirteenth-century reign was a critical period for the unification of Spain despite his own political setbacks. Finally, one of the largest language reforms ever was essentially the invention of two Norwegian written languages early in the twentieth century. Officially, the major reforms affecting spelling occurred in 1907 and 1917, soon after the country ended its union with Sweden in 1905.

Social upheaval, revolution, and attempts to nationalize and control a population—it cannot be coincidence these often coincide with linguistic reforms. Russia certainly has seen several reforms that met with some success, the first coordinated by Peter the Great, who realized literacy in one language would promote national unity—a strategy used by King Alfred the Great during the Old English period. Under the Soviets, massive language and spelling reforms were initiated by Vladimir Lenin soon after the 1917 revolution; as part of the reforms, four troublesome letters were purged. In the years that followed, the government sponsored these linguistic campaigns to bring unity and a sense of social identity to disparate peoples, as well as to solidify Russian control under Joseph Stalin.

A year after the overthrow of its monarchy in 1910, the Portuguese enjoyed a particularly successful and logical reform of spelling, unmercifully eliminating most needless double consonants and Greek spellings that had silent letters. Unfortunately, Portugal and Brazil, where Portuguese is the first language for most of the population, have struggled ever since the 1911 reform to bring their orthographies into greater alignment. Portuguese-speaking nations have attempted several official agreements on the matter, but with little effect, especially in Brazil.

Despite the logic and transparency of Portuguese spelling, a study published in the *British Journal of Psychology* examined thirteen European orthographies and found that Portuguese—along with French, Danish, and in particular English—posed the greatest difficulties for children who are learning to read. Philip Seymor, professor of psychology at the University of Dundee in Scotland, and his fellow researchers in Finland found, however, that it is not merely the inconsistency of English spelling that poses difficulties for readers. In their study of children's spelling skills, English itself has a type of "syllabic complexity" that creates additional problems many other languages do not face in terms of sound/letter relationships. In other words, part of the problem of learning English spelling deals with trying to master various complexities of modern English speech. A spelling reform, then, might need to change our speech patterns as well as our alphabet.

In Great Britain and the United States, organized reforms of spelling have seldom occurred during the watershed moments when the nations were reinventing themselves. In fact, the only major planned reform that significantly changed English spelling, not to mention language, goes all the way back to King Alfred during the ninth century. Even so, his Wessex standard was eclipsed by the language of Norman invaders, who certainly changed English but not in a planned manner and not with the intent of creating a consistent English orthography. Likewise, Orm in the 1200s provided many improvements to English spelling, though his was not a planned reform but rather an organic, gradual adoption of his spelling conventions by other writers. More than two hundred years later, King Henry IV and his son helped replace French with English as the official language of England—dovetailing language reform with solidifying their power. They did little, however, in terms of reforming the spelling system.

In the first half of the fifteenth century, Chancery scribes moved forward with these kings' efforts through an organized attempt to establish a standard based on a London dialect. Yet, even this officious group did not seem to realize the scope of what they were doing, providing a standard not just for royalty and court but also for merchants, schools, and common people in general. More important, the scribes seemed content to draw for the most part on particular existing spellings rather than devising a more logical and coherent spelling system.

I believe the last opportunity in England for a structured reform of spelling occurred during the time of Richard Mulcaster. In the late 1500s, the pedagogue Mulcaster was fairly successful in developing rules for spelling, not just altering selective words here and there. His was clearly a planned reform of spelling, one that still affects many modern spellings. Mulcaster's success must largely be due to the fact that the English Renaissance, with its emphasis on literature, was in full bloom—not to mention that England was enjoying its so-called golden age during the rule of Queen Elizabeth I. The time was ripe for a major reform of spelling, yet Mulcaster's compromises resulted in helpful but limited changes. Neither did Her Majesty, despite writing poems and other works, seem intent on establishing order within English orthography, focusing instead on providing economic, political, and religious order within the country.

Spelling Reforms in America

In America, reformists have been plentiful and vocal, but their successes have been stymied more by bad timing than by the lack of a plan. The one exception might be Noah Webster, who accomplished the most successful reform of American English orthography. He saw many of his reformed spellings take hold in America. Others would become widely accepted only decades after his death, as part of a more natural type of language change rather than part of the quick reform Webster once wanted.

In the 1780s, Noah Webster wrote an influential and enormously successful textbook, *Elementary Spelling Book*, usually called the *Blue Back Speller*, which has been in print ever since. Some twenty years later when Webster was in his early forties, he began work that would lead to the most influential of American dictionaries, and he finished his masterpiece in 1828 at the age of seventy. The title, *American Dictionary of the English Language*, suggests his nationalistic purpose: to provide sensible spellings distinct from British English, even though he clearly drew on Samuel Johnson's British dictionary published years earlier. Technically, *American Dictionary* is still published, but only as a reproduction of Webster's original. Contrary to common belief, the term "Webster's dictionary" for well over a hundred years has not referred to any one dictionary, despite the extensive legal and publicity efforts of Merriam-Webster, Inc.

Webster himself lobbied actively for copyright laws, but his own name has long been legally appropriated by many publishers.

Viewing spelling as a moral matter, Webster worked on his dictionary with the same evangelical passion he would use in devising his own translation of the Bible. His dictionary would reflect this dual fervor in the way he included many terms and definitions based on the Bible. In defining *hell*, for example, he drew upon biblical phrases such as "pains of hell," "gates of hell," and the Hebrew term *sheol*. To be fair, Webster provided Greek references as well and noted *hell* also means "a place into which a tailor throws his shreds." He also defines *marriage* as "instituted by God himself for the purpose of preventing the promiscuous intercourse of the sexes." (Although not unique to Christianity of his time, in defining *sex* Webster states that "the male sex is usually characterized by muscular strength, boldness and firmness," while "the female sex is characterized by softness, sensibility and modesty." Dictionaries now avoid blatant political incorrectness, yet *Merriam-Webster's* still maintains that the "gentle sex" is the female gender.)

In an essay written in 1789 on the need for spelling reform, it is difficult to tell if Webster is discussing how to be a God-fearing Christian or how to save writers from their slothful misspellings:

> Indolence is another obstacle to improvements. The most arduous task a reformer has to execute, is to make people think; to rouse them from that lethargy, which, like the mantle of sleep, covers them in repose and contentment.

Like his biblical namesake, Noah Webster embarked on a long, arduous task seeking to preserve as well as change his world. Yet unlike the Noah of ark-building fame, Webster was surrounded by many others who shared his conviction, if not the actual work. Few people in the government of this new nation, however, proactively implemented Noah's beliefs, perhaps because they failed to understand the galvanizing power of language.

Webster's colleague Benjamin Franklin had argued earlier for sweeping changes of English orthography, including reconstructing the alphabet itself. Webster drew heavily on Franklin's ideas regarding what improvements might be needed. Ben Franklin had even written his own tongue-in-cheek (or glass-in-hand) dictionary. This founding father is, after all, the man who said, "Beer is proof that God loves us and wants us to be happy." Offering scores of slang terms for being intoxicated, his *Drinker's Dictionary* includes sadly forgotten colonial gems such as "Bewitch'd," "Wasted his Paunch," and "He sees two Moons." Franklin, as an admirer of fine wine, would later serve as ambassador to France and surely must have acquired additional synonyms there as part of his linguistic research.

American memories of the Revolutionary War were still fresh when Noah Webster began writing dictionaries around the turn of the century (he published a relatively brief one in 1806). Thomas Jefferson, so much a symbol of American philosophy during the war, was president at the time Webster was researching and publishing his dictionary, and Webster himself had served in the war for a brief time. For years after the war, Webster worked diligently to promote the new centralized government of the United States. His work included writing pamphlets in favor of a constitution. Webster, like other Americans, knew it would take more than a piece of paper to rouse the former colonists into a single nation. He realized the letters that Americans used on pieces of paper could themselves help bring about unity. His patriotic zeal is evident in a 1789 essay arguing for an immediate reform of American spellings:

Let us then seize the present moment and establish a national language as well as a national government. . . .

As an independent people, our reputation abroad demands that, in all things, we should be federal; be national. . . . In short, let it be impressed upon the mind of every American, that to neglect the means of commanding respect abroad, is treason against the character and dignity of a brave independent people.

Maybe the coming fin de siècle added to Webster's anxieties about the nation's future, but his decades-long passion finally culminated in 1828 with a two-volume dictionary having some seventy thousand words, twelve thousand more than any other dictionary up to then.

Ironically, the most influential dictionary in American history did not sell well after its first few years. George and Charles Merriam bought the rights when Webster died, hence the claim of Merriam-Webster, Inc., to publishing the "true" Webster's dictionary. In contrast, Webster's *Blue Back Book* taught spelling to generations of Americans before and after the author's death. The book industry tends to list this speller as the number three bestselling book of all time (behind the *Holy Bible* and *Quotations from Chairman Mao*) with sales at approximately one hundred million copies. Still, Webster's dictionary would be equally influential in changing American spellings, if for no other reason than the fact that for many decades *American Dictionary of the English Language* would be plagiarized by a series of successful imitators.

One reason why Webster's crusade was a systematic reform is that he did not arbitrarily select words he deemed in need of change. Nor were his respellings inconsistent. Although he frequently revised words that seemed idiosyncratic in their spelling (he succeeded in replacing Anglo-Norman *joal* with *jail*), the lexicographer focused on ten specific patterns and attempted to reform them in a consistent manner. Most of the bothersome patterns he detected dealt with word endings. His planned renovations included the following:

- Changing words ending in *-our* to *-or*
- Deleting final *-k* when silent
- Using *ee* rather than *ea* for the long <e> sound
- Using *-er* rather than the outdated *-re* to represent <er> (Perhaps as a reminder of how different they are, people in the theater business still cling to *theatre*.)

Even though his own etymologies were sometimes incorrect, Webster also hoped to eliminate the "pseudoclassical" spellings erroneously given during the English Renaissance. In fact, Webster frequently would base pronunciations, spellings, and definitions on what he considered the Anglo-Saxon heritage or the language of the common people (for instance, he defended the use of the double negative, as in "I have not seen nobody").

Unfortunately, most Americans accepted his specific respellings on a case-by-case basis, therefore increasing the inconsistency of spelling as a whole. Take, for instance, Webster's campaign against silent letters. In America at least, he won the battle involving words such as *music*, *check*, and *color* (formerly known as *musick*, *cheque*, and *colour*). He lost when it came to replacing *examine*, *thumb*, and *isle* with *examin*, *thum*, and *ile*. The spelling *ax* seems his only victory against silent *e*, although *axe* is considered equally correct.

This greatest of American spelling reforms was not entirely successful. In terms of the larger picture of rules for American spelling, the inconsistencies actually increased in some instances. Some words subscribed to Webster's rules, while others having the same pattern adhered to pre-Webster rules. Still, as a whole, we can fairly say that Webster's spellings made spelling easier, more logical, and more consistent for Americans. From a reformist perspective, the greatest shortcoming is that his dictionary was conservative in terms of the changes it offered, especially when compared with the reformist ideas Webster promoted before 1800.

Did he mellow in his middle and late years—or become jaded about the possibility of success? The one neologism Webster added to his dictionary was *demoralize*. Possibly, this concept was much with him during long years of combating the juggernaut of irregular spellings. Yet he never gave up the cause, revising his own dictionary not long before he died at the age of eighty-five. Possibly, he was overly timid when it came to implementing reforms rather than just arguing about them. We should also note that his translation of the Bible was still a conservative translation based on the existing King James version, despite his arguments that it was flawed. Most likely, he simply came to the belief that language changes must occur gradually, despite his earlier, strident arguments to the contrary.

In 1837, Horace Greeley, who later became influential editor of the *New York Tribune*, wrote Webster and noted his disappointment that his dictionary did not go far enough in reforming spellings. Webster replied forthrightly, "I deviate as little as possible from usage." Webster had in fact expressed his orthographic conservatism from the very start of the project. In 1808, he wrote the following in regard to the duties of the lexicographer: "No great changes should ever be made at once, nor should any change be made which violates established principles." This was also near the time when Webster became particularly religious and convinced that his fellow Americans needed Christian guidance. Possibly, Noah's newfound devotion to traditional religious values made him rethink the need for a major and sudden linguistic revolution.

Whatever the reason, Webster's reforms improved the logic of numerous spellings, yet the major problems involving letter/sound relationships remained. The timing seemed right when compared to the success of other language and spelling reforms throughout history. America was still a fledgling nation, not only forming its national identity but seemingly trying to prove it was independent from Great Britain. The War of 1812 was a painful reminder of the differences between the two cultures. A declaration of orthographic independence, one going beyond Webster's conservative reforms, would have seemed appropriate. Foreign affairs aside, language reform also serves to unify divided people, and the American states of Webster's time were far from unified, especially due to controversies involving slavery and states' rights. Webster's name wielded unsurpassed clout in America in terms of all matters lexical and orthographic; his spelling textbooks alone had established that matter.

Yet the moment passed, leaving us with a shadow of the reforms needed. I do not believe Webster's moderation alone can be blamed for the lack of a more significant reform during his time. Americans were still wedded to English culture despite vicious wars, geographic distance, and political differences. Compare the situation to how the English for centuries would depend on and borrow from the French language— despite their wars and apparent dislike of one another. Earlier, the Anglo-Saxons had borrowed heavily from the language of Vikings who successfully invaded Britain. As often happens, even wars and strife are not sufficient to keep people from sharing and borrowing words or spellings. Webster's America focused its energies on creating its separate identity in terms of government, religion, and economics—much more so than in terms of a drastically improved orthography.

In addition, the United States also lacked the sort of authoritative figure comparable to, say, King Alfred of England, King Alfonso of Spain, or President Atatürk of Turkey. Webster might have been *the* American spelling authority of his time, but prestige alone is rarely sufficient to institute a reform. The idea of a language academy for America had been tossed around during Webster's day. In 1780, John Adams futilely encouraged Congress to develop what he called the "American Academy for Refining, Improving, and Ascertaining the English Language." Around 1820, there was somewhat greater success with the American Academy of Language and Belles Lettres (apparently, Webster's ideas concerning -*re* endings had not kicked in). Even with John Quincy Adams and other dignitaries holding office, this organization soon expired, having focused largely on noting the literary accomplishments of Americans. Thomas Jefferson, who appreciated the need for language reform despite being an inconsistent speller himself, declined to serve as honorary president of the organization.

Thus, Webster's early ideas on reforming spelling did not obtain sufficient political support, at least not enough to encourage the government-sponsored reforms such as those that have succeeded elsewhere. But wouldn't we have needed a markedly different type of American government for it to have instituted a powerful language-regulating agency?

Consider Peter the Great. Not having to work through a committee structure, this czar was able to implement a highly successful reform of Russian orthography. The same power and resolve that helped Peter succeed as a linguistic reformer also allowed him to cut off the head of his wife's lover and preserve it in a jar, which stayed in her bedroom until the czar died in 1725. My point is not that we should avoid irritating spelling reformers. We just need to realize that spelling reforms require much more authority and control than most people understand, and a successful major reform normally requires a government structure enjoying more power than Americans might want to give it. True, democratic nations such as Germany of the 1990s have attempted language reforms, but the most successful have occurred when autocratic powers such as czars, kings, and dictators are ultimately in charge of language reform.

Today, *Merriam-Webster's Dictionary* might trace its lineage to Webster's original work, but no major dictionary since his time ever took on the responsibility of changing American orthography. In fact, several dictionaries of the modern era have shunned the notion of being the guardians of language at all, declaring their lexical responsibility is to describe rather than prescribe language choices. In the 1960s, *Webster's Third International Dictionary* led the way in taking this un-Webster-like approach—labeled by some critics as "permissiveness."

Drawing on Noah Webster's ideas for spelling reform, the true successors of Webster would appear not long after the Civil War.

The Heirs to Webster

More clout than we might think is needed to overhaul American spellings. Even President Theodore Roosevelt, of big-stick fame and the man who reformed powerful monopolies and railroad corporations, met his match trying to reform spelling. He was aware of the problems of learning to spell, for his own skills were not strong. Roosevelt was but one of many members of his generation who tried to reform spelling. His efforts, coming again around the turn of a century, grew out of a larger international movement.

The Civil War, along with tensions that led up to it and came afterward, left little time for revising the American spelling system, but the years from approximately 1875 to 1915 were glory days for Americans and British who wanted to rant against orthography—not that their ranting accomplished a great deal.

Several organizations joined the rally. In 1876, the American Philological Association, a key organization for academics of the time, promoted the idea, as did a convention at the Centennial Exposition in Philadelphia. This interest soon launched the Spelling Reform Association and, in 1906, the Simplified Spelling Board. In 1898, the National Education Association modestly jumped on the bandwagon by endorsing about a dozen respellings that had been suggested (of these, the only major success in America was *program*, which had been unsuccessfully struggling for decades to be accepted in Great Britain).

These reformists were not the assorted nonconformists of today who picket spelling bees. Members and supporters of the reforms of 1875 to 1915 included Theodore Roosevelt, philosopher William James, poet laureate Alfred Tennyson, Mark Twain, Charles Darwin, playwright George Bernard Shaw, and industrial titan Andrew Carnegie, whose fortune helped fund the Spelling Reform Association (which diminished quickly and significantly when his checks stopped coming). Noah Webster's legacy survived with these reformers, for most of their suggested respellings could be traced to his reformist essays, textbooks, and dictionary. In fact, these reformers had their greatest success in helping solidify some of Webster's spellings that had gradually been gaining acceptance in America.

This time, spelling reforms received considerable support from people with influence, yet even this did not help. In 1906, President Teddy Roosevelt presided over the greatest debacle in the history of American spelling reforms when he overestimated the power he had over not only the language but also the government. By executive order, the Government Printing Office (essentially, Chancery scribes of Roosevelt's time) was told to adopt some three hundred respellings recommended by the Simplified Spelling Board, including *thru* for *through*. Later, Roosevelt would blame that one respelling for the collapse of his initiative, but other words meeting resistance included *dropt* (*dropped*), *envelop* (*envelope*), and *altho* (*although*).

Roosevelt's initiatives would have eventually affected spellings used by the legislative and judicial branches of government as well. As influential as Roosevelt was in other aspects of his presidency, his enthusiasm (or, put another way, his arrogance) managed to alienate even his allies. Never mind that Americans had already largely accepted at least half of the gang of three hundred respellings, including *center*, *valor*, *hiccup*, and *jail*. Amid loud protests and considerable reprinting of documents that had used the new spellings, Congress and the Supreme Court declared they would not go along with Roosevelt's campaign "to make our spelling a little less foolish." The newspapers viciously assaulted the revisions, perhaps perceiving this Roosevelt reform as hitting too close to home by assaulting orthography. Indeed, people were not so much concerned with just these three hundred words. After all, how many people wrote *glycerin*, *paleography*, or *pedobaptist*? A larger concern was that if the president could change spellings of these, then he would establish the right to change the tens of thousands of other words in English.

In what seems a rare Roosevelt move, the president soon rescinded his order, and the new spellings were recalled.

In Roosevelt's defense, the president realized from the beginning that the reformed spellings would require public approval. Sounding more like Forrest Gump than a Rough Rider, Roosevelt stated that without public support the spellings should "be dropt, and that is all there is about it." The president's head of the printing office was the one who extended the initiative beyond just the printing done for executive departments. However, the president surely proved a more interesting target than a governmental printer. The idea of irrepressible Teddy Roosevelt throwing his presidential weight against slender letters of American spellings provided ample fodder for cartoonists, reporters, and politicians with an ax to grind (or axe, if you prefer to avoid one of the many "Roosevelt respellings" that today are acceptable).

As history shows, language reforms usually need someone with authority to implement change, and Roosevelt could have been that person—if he had been president a hundred years earlier. Despite the proliferation of powerful voices and intellectual support between 1875 and 1915, the majority of Americans and government leaders were not linguistically pliable at this point in history. Americans were too attached to their existing ways and to the democratic notion that spelling reform is not a power granted to any branch of government.

In some ways, the spelling reform was a major signal to the executive branch about the limits of its powers. Roosevelt firmly believed the president could essentially do whatever was deemed best for the public unless these actions were clearly prohibited by the Constitution. This can be a dangerous assumption. Prior to 1906, Roosevelt exercised considerable power in various aspects of American life, such as conservation, foreign policy, trust busting, and racial equality. By standing up to the presidential assumption that the alphabet was also under executive purview, the other two branches of government, along with the public, showed there were limits to even a president's authority.

The public embarrassment over what we might today call "Spellinggate" proved a grave setback for reformists. Roosevelt managed to put the issue before Congress in a way that made it impossible for legislators to separate the general idea of reforming spelling (a goal many favored) from Roosevelt's political ideology. In its debates over the respellings, Congress considered the larger implications of power and had to dismiss the need for spelling reforms.

The entire incident showed America how undemocratic a spelling reform can be when it is made *for* the people but not *by* the people. Given the momentum of the movement, though, the reforms did not cease immediately. Along with the sword rattling in Europe heralding World War I, the last straw was Carnegie's decision in 1915 to end his financial support.

Since that era, the last attempt at reform meeting with any success (and it was not much) occurred during the Great Depression when the *Chicago Tribune* announced it would use eighty reformed spellings. The paper had been sympathetic with the cause since the 1870s, and around 1935 it began an experiment that would last four decades. The respellings, many of which had appeared on other lists popular with reformers, included several that are not particularly startling and in fact are considered permissible options, such as *intern*. Others seem more alarming, including *agast, jaz, traffic,* and *thoro*.

By 1939, the list would be pared by about half, with attrition increasingly taking toll as the paper quietly dropped one word or another for years. In 1975, the paper called the whole thing quits in an article entitled *"Thru is through and so is tho,"* apologizing that the reformed spellings had created problems for students whose teachers preferred the traditional spellings. Even in the early 1970s, the simplified spellings could scarcely be found within the *Tribune*, unless they had been accepted already by the public as alternate spellings. The article claimed it would still refrain from a few *-ogue* words by using *epilog, dialog,* and *synagog*, yet the paper turned its back on these as well.

The *Tribune* cannot take credit for any real success. Even alternate spellings such as *catalog* were widely used before the paper embraced them. Hardly any publisher followed the *Tribune* in promoting the respellings. This last — but very long —

gasp of the turn-of-the-century reforms amounts to little more than a stubborn denial of the movement's waning influence, and perhaps the *Chicago Tribune*'s as well.

One overlooked problem with the entire movement is that the reformist strategy focused almost exclusively on lists, whether the list was a dozen words or three hundred. On the positive side, this approach allowed reformists to focus on what people might consider the worst offenders—egregious examples of spellings that fail to reflect how people pronounce the words. Apparently, the premise was that most Americans would be just as scandalized by these examples as were the reformers, yet such was not the case—especially in the case of a "top three hundred" list as opposed to a more manageable number. The reformists assumed that if Americans would first accept even just a dozen words, then the rest of the lexicon could follow. Perhaps, but it is just as likely that a piecemeal approach would do exactly what we have seen with words such as *dialog* and *ax*. These reformed spellings have merely increased inconsistency by adding another valid way of spelling *dialogue* and *axe*.

Suppose you are in charge of an automated assembly line that puts ketchup into those annoying foil bags (or sachets, if you believe they deserve the French-derived name)—the ones dispersed at Burger King and other fine establishments. If you find that each day 20 percent of the bags are seriously over- or understuffed with fancy ketchup, would you be satisfied in merely replacing the defects at the end of each workday? Surely, it would be more effective to deal with the real source of the problem: the machinery that turns out the product.

Similarly, a reformer who wants to fix spelling should focus on the "machinery" that produces errant spellings—the larger system of rules and conventions. Throughout history, the most successful reforms—as with Korean, Finnish, and Turkish—

did not target particular misspellings. Rather, these successes focused on larger rules that dictate how to spell, on an entire alphabet, or on the development of a "book language."

I am not unsympathetic to current reformers' arguments, but I for one prefer to focus on goals that can actually be accomplished within a lifetime or two. Overhauling the system is the only effective means of reforming English spelling, yet history indicates we have missed that opportunity. Perhaps another one will come when America, the United Kingdom, or another English-speaking nation seriously reinvents itself or adopts a new national language having a more consistent orthography. I am content to watch a few spellings morph their way into new, and sometimes better, versions as a result of popular usage—though I will forever swing my red-ink pen to cleave *alot* into *a lot*—even should that dreadful day arrive when dictionaries succumb to the people's will. I have told my students that using *alot* is like writing *alittle* or *abunch*. That worked until I recently started seeing students show up using *alittle* in their writing.

Surely, the apocalypse is upon us.

Americanisms, Britishisms, and Otherisms

One effect of the American reforms is they helped the troublesome differences between American spellings and those of most of the rest of the English-speaking world. American spellers need to be aware of these differences, especially those spellings used in America and the lands that are now, or formerly were a part of, the United Kingdom (U.K.). The fact that Americans see these U.K. spellings, especially on the Internet, makes it even more difficult to acquire spelling skills that reflect American spellings. As mentioned earlier in this book, the differences between American and U.K. spellings also make it even more difficult to reform our spelling systems. If American spellings alone were changed, we would be sadly mistaken to assume the rest of the world would get in line at the bookstore to learn how they could spell just like us.

Anyone trying to list or neatly categorize these differences faces the inevitable problem of oversimplifying. For instance, the terms "United Kingdom spellings," "English spellings," and "Commonwealth spellings" are not synonymous, and many of the so-called American spellings will frequently be found as alternate choices in other countries. Still, we know the American spellings can differ from those used elsewhere, so I wish to cover some of the major issues and problems.

The Irish writer George Bernard Shaw once said that "England and America are two countries divided by a common language." This might seem outrageous, but perhaps the idea has more truth than we might think. During World War II, both governments developed dictionaries so soldiers could better communicate with their allies. One such text was *It's a Piece of Cake! RAF Slang Made Easy*, intended to help American aviators understand the particular vocabulary used within the Royal Air Force.

In terms of spelling, the differences between American and British English are not as great as those between cricket and baseball (or between English beer and the sweet, carbonated fluids sold in American bars). Still, the orthographical differences have led to problems for spellers in an era of increasing global communication. Even if both the Americans and British agree to measure things in meters, we will still bicker on whether to spell it *meter* or *metre*.

Following are the major ways in which American spellings currently differ from those found in the United Kingdom, although the British are increasingly apt to accept Americanized spellings as viable options.

- **-our reduction:** Approximately three dozen U.K. nouns ending in *-our* are simplified to *-or*.

  U.S.: *honor, armor, harbor*   U.K.: *honour, armour, harbour*

  Preferred in both nations, *glamour* is an exception; the *-or* of *glamorous* is preferred as well. The United States keeps *-our* in words not making the <er> sound (*devour*, *detour*).

- **-er endings:** In America, many British nouns ending in *-re* are changed to *-er*.

  U.S.: *fiber, saber, center*   U.K.: *fibre, sabre, centre*

  This preference also deals with the <er> sound as heard in America, so words like *genre* and *acquire* are not affected. Several <er> words missed out on the change, including *antre*, *acre*, *cadastre*, *chancre*, and *nacre*. Most are rare terms or predictably end in *-cre*.

- **-ize and -yze verbs:** Americans prefer *-ze* endings rather than *-ise* and *-yse*.

  U.S.: *penalize, recognize, analyze*   U.K.: *penalise, recognise, analyse*

  Several exceptions exist on both sides of the pond; *surprise*, *comprise*, and *demise* have only one spelling in both nations. Only a dozen words in America end with the *-yze* suffix, but the *-ize* ending affects many verbs and is also a handy way to form a neologism in the United States (e.g., *bagonize*, to wait for your bags at the airport). The *-ize* spelling is actually the older, "truer" British version, which was changed because of French influence in late Middle and early Modern English.

- *ae* and *oe* reduction: The Latin or Greek *ae* and *oe* in British words are reduced to *e* in America if the *a* or *o* is silent.

  U.S.: *medieval, maneuver, fetus*   U.K.: *mediaeval, manoeuvre, foetus*

  In America, a few such terms can be spelled either way, such as *amoeba* or *ameba*.

- *-ogue* reduction: In America, most words ending with Latin or Greek *-ogue* are simplified to *-og*.

  U.S.: *dialog, catalog, analog*   U.K.: *dialogue, catalogue, analogue*

  Again, exceptions occur. In both nations, *pedagogue* is much more common than *pedagog*, while *epilogue* and *epilog* are both accepted in the United States.

- deletion of other silent vowels: At the end of a syllable, Americans are more apt to drop a silent *e* (or the rare silent *u*). This preference is especially true when *g* precedes the silent vowel.

  U.S.: *routing, fledgling, judgment*   U.K.: *routeing, fledgeling, judgement*

- *-st* reduction: U.K. words ending with *-st* are normally simplified in America.

  U.S.: *amid, among, while*   U.K.: *amidst, amongst, whilst*

  Some argue there are different shades of meaning between *among* versus *amongst* and other such pairs. However, the U.K. spellings are becoming rare, going the way of *betwixt, hast,* and *wouldst.*

- ***-ed* rather than *-t* verbs:** In America, past-tense verbs are rarely spelled with a *-t* as long as *-ed* is an option.

  U.S.: *spelled, learned, spoiled* U.K.: *spelt, learnt, spoilt*

  A few American verbs such as *burnt* and *knit* are just as acceptable as *burned* and *knitted*. In general, the more commonly used a verb is, the more it has resisted being changed to the *-ed* spelling, especially *slept, left,* and *kept*. For no clear reason, the British actually prefer *lighted* to *lit,* though the preference is the opposite in the United States.

- ***-ense* nouns:** Some nouns ending in *-ence* are changed to *-ense* in America.

  U.S.: *offense, pretense, defense* U.K.: *offence, pretence, defence*

  This preference is inconsistent and leads to numerous misspellings. In America, the *-ence* ending is actually preferred for nouns that can also be used as a verb, as in "I must practice" (verb) versus "I missed the practice" (noun).

- **"double *l*" verbs:** This is the most complex and least dependable difference despite the numerous words the pattern affects. In the United Kingdom, a verb having a vowel plus an *l* undergoes a doubling of the *l* when a new ending (such as *-er*) is added. In America, though, many such verbs keep the single *l*.

  U.S.: *traveler, equaled, signaling* U.K.: *traveller, equalled, signalling*

  The American "nondoubling" preference has several exceptions, such as *speller, annulled,* and *appalled*. Some can be explained by the fact that the pattern is determined by where the stress is in the word and by the type of vowel coming before or after *l*. Yet even these caveats do not explain all exceptions. The Brits also prefer to double other consonants in verbs when a suffix is added (*worshipped*), while Americans often prefer or tolerate the single consonant (*worshiped*). The lack of consistency in doubling consonants in either nation poses one of the greatest challenges to spellers everywhere.

Other spelling differences defy categorization. Sometimes, they merely reflect how the same word might be pronounced in America as opposed to Britain. At other times, the American variant evolved from an attempt to simplify spelling. Here are a few examples that, while not always idiosyncratic, do not neatly fit the previous categories. Keep in mind these are just tendencies; writers in both nations are often confused about which form is preferred in their own country.

AMERICAN	UNITED KINGDOM
airplane	aeroplane
aluminum	aluminium
behoove	behove
Briticism	Britishism
carburetor	carburettor or carburetter
check	cheque
chili	chilli
cozy	cosy
dispatch	despatch
furor	furore
gray	grey
lasagna	lasagnea
licorice	liquorice
mustache	moustache
omelet	omelette

pajamas	pyjamas
plow	plough
specialty	speciality
tire	tyre
toward	towards
vial	phial
yogurt	yoghurt

A few differences are decreasing or have already become negligible. At one time, for instance, the *-xion* ending was common in British spellings, as with *connexion*. Nowadays, spellings such as *connection* are far more common around the globe. Even *jail* seems to be usurping *gaol* in England.

Americans seem both proud of their lexical distinctness and insecure at the same time. For instance, we gravitate toward *-t* endings when we try to be poetic or haughty ("I dreamt of frolicking amongst the forgotten letters and runes of history"). In terms of American universities at least, perhaps the surest way to miss a job opportunity is to refer to your application as a mere *résumé*; it should be called a *vitae*, as befitting the pedagogues chambered within the lofty halls of academe. The spelling *vita* is moderately acceptable unless you are applying to teach classical languages.

The limited success of Noah Webster and his heirs nudged American orthography away from the spellings of Great Britain. Webster wanted our spellings to differ as a means of establishing an American identity, as well as improving sound/letter relationships in at least our part of the world. (He also believed the American printing industry would benefit from spelling reforms, for Webster claimed no English press would deign to publish Americans' writing if it meant having to use American spellings.)

Americans' linguistic uniqueness creates communication problems with more than Great Britain. Across the world, many former U.K. colonies use English as a major language, and their standard resembles the British standard more than the American. The term "Commonwealth English" is a general term used to refer to this variety of English, which in theory differs little from "British English" as used in Great Britain.

Australia is the best-known example, but even in nations where English is not the official or most widely used language, Commonwealth English is extremely important in commerce and government—as is the case in Nigeria, Pakistan, and India, which is the second-most-populated country in the world. Other sites using Commonwealth spellings include Hong Kong, Uganda, South Africa, Egypt, New Zealand, Belize, Malta, Singapore, Trinidad, Kenya, and the Falkland Islands. The United Nations and the European Union also prefer Commonwealth spellings.

When using terms such as "American English" or "Commonwealth English," we imply more homogeneity than there really is. Each English-speaking nation has developed its own take on English, including spellings. Commonwealth member Canada is a prime example, for sometimes it is difficult to say if the Canadian spellings of English terms are more similar to British or American spellings. Often, it depends on where you are in Canada because of regional preferences in that nation. In general, Canadians prefer many American spellings such as *encyclopedia*, *curb*, *organize* (and other *-ize* instead of *-ise* spellings), *program*, *tire*, *draft*, and *airplane*. However, most Canadians prefer certain British endings: *-our* rather than *-or* (*neighbour*); *-ce* rather than *-se* for nouns (*licence*); and *-re* rather than *-er* (*centre*).

Of course, the influence of American economics, culture, and politics will continue to introduce American ideas and spellings around the world, even in places that historically have preferred Commonwealth English. Do not underestimate the power of spell-checkers either. The United States dominates the production of this technology, and even though most spell-checkers sold overseas will allow users to draw on Common-wealth spellings, the default dictionary is almost always based on the American orthography preferred by a growing number of international businesses, industries, and organizations.

When English was finally deemed worthy of rules and conventions, our spellings were standardized unevenly, and no authoritative entity was able to step up to the plate and rally the consensus needed to create a more logical, regular system. With the possible exceptions of Richard Mulcaster and Noah Webster, Chancery scribes are the closest English has had in terms of such an authority since the Norman invasion.

At this stage in American and English history, the chances of a spelling reform are so slight we would be better off spending our time and energy mastering how to spell using our existing system. In short, we need to work with what we have, not waste time on futile reforms.

Why We Misspell

To improve our ability to drive a car safely, it helps to understand why automobile accidents occur, as a police officer told a defensive-driving class I attended upon receiving a well-deserved ticket. To improve our spelling, it similarly helps to understand why spelling mishaps occur.

Or perhaps the causes are beyond our control. Several individuals have told me that "good spellers are born, not made." Too often, this reasoning is merely an excuse for not doing the hard work of trying to improve one's spelling. No doubt, scientists have found or are close to finding all manners of genes associated with language—ranging from dyslexia to the ability to intentionally write backward. On one hand, I am excited by such research and the possibilities of understanding relationships among biology, heredity, cognition, and language. On the other hand, a naive understanding of this research makes it even more tempting for some people to give up on spelling (not to mention reading and writing) if they can blame it all on their genes.

People can substantially alter their spelling ability. In one of the few longitudinal studies of spelling ability, Wayne MacDonald and Anne Cornwall, psychologists at IWK Children's

Hospital in Nova Scotia, found that spelling achievement scores of a group of six-year-olds did not predict the spelling skills of these same students eleven years later. Although it is not clear why some students improved or became poorer with spelling, the study revealed their skills were neither preset nor immune to change. If such a thing as a "natural" spelling ability exists, this ability can still increase, become stable, or decline. Many people with severe dyslexia, for example, find strategies that improve their spelling abilities.

In short, *maybe* genes and biology can predispose us to spell effectively or otherwise, but that does not mean we either have it or we don't.

Questionable Assumptions

Everyone who has ever misspelled a word can tell his or her unique story about why these errors occurred. We each have our own faults and blind spots in regard to spelling, and some writing situations are going to be more conducive to misspellings than others. In other words, there are many reasons why a person will misspell from one day to the next. And each of us has a unique background and set of spelling demons that make one person's reasons for misspelling not quite like mine or anyone else's.

That being said, patterns and tendencies do exist. Otherwise, I would never bother, in this book or in a classroom, giving advice about spelling. The problem is that spelling is so complex we cannot point to just one or two causes of misspellings, despite the claims of purported quick-fix remedies that fool parents and teachers into thinking, "If we just fix [fill in the blank], everyone can be a good speller."

Let's take a brief look at five common assumptions that are either false or tend to be blown out of proportion to some truths they might actually reflect. The assumptions are so questionable that I will put them in the form of questions so they do not have the appearance of fact. These ideas are not 100 percent wrong, so afterward I want to distill valid concerns and solutions from these assumptions.

Are people confused about how to spell because they are inundated with "cutely misspelled" brand names such as "U-Haul," "Shop Rite," "Toys 'R' Us," and "Xtreme Racing"?

No, the worst aspect of these proper nouns is they are based on an annoying, unimaginative advertising gimmick.

Many people like to assault the lords of commerce for their flagrant and deliberate disregard of correct spelling. These intentional misspellings (and I am referring to those resulting from a marketing ploy, not from ignorance) are easy targets given their visibility. The fact that we are bothered by these misspellings only confirms they succeed in getting the consumer's attention. As often as I have heard people bemoan such deliberate misspellings, never once have I seen this annoyance stop anyone from making a purchase with the cacographic culprits.

Fact: a child or adult who regularly sees a misspelling is more likely to produce it. That is why many English teachers will tell you about an ironic job hazard: their spelling skills tend to suffer as a result of marking so many misspellings in students' papers. (The problem is strangely limited to spelling and using irregular verbs correctly, so you can still trust an English teacher's judgment about commas and misplaced modifiers.)

Nonetheless, there are at least two reasons why deliberate misspellings on signs and labels rarely have an ill effect on a person's spelling ability. First, most of these use correct spellings, so as a whole signs and labels help more than hurt people in terms of spelling. If you are looking for misspelled slogans and brand names, you will surely find them, but they are the exceptions rather than the rule. For every *'n* you find in a "Shop 'n Go," there are scores of public *and*s elsewhere. I would wager that the ampersand (&) is nearly as common in signs as *and*, yet it rarely carries over into most people's formal writing.

Second, we learn early on that businesses—not to mention today's musical performers (the term *musicians* is not always accurate)—assume it is their artistic right to misspell their names. Children learn quickly in life they do not have this privilege until they grow up to be ad writers or pop-music icons. Intuitively, young readers realize our spelling rules do not consistently apply to signposts and brand names.

In some instances, it is almost impossible to miss the nonstandard "wackiness" of these misspellings, as if the sign were also saying, "Hey boys and girls, look at how crazzzzzy OUR name is!" This is a cue that the spelling is not quite normal. Take, for example, the "Toys 'R' Us" name—bright, whimsical letters that look like balloons, while the *R* often faces backward to show how different it is from all the right-facing *R*'s of the world. The letters are slightly jumbled as well, as if written by a precocious, playful child. If this store's name were a child, in fact, it would surely run with scissors.

Through assorted context clues, children naturally learn there are different forms of literacy and different types of spelling. The anomaly of misspelled store names can help people gain a healthy distrust of the orthography of signs, if not of advertising in general. The most indignant reactions to deliberate misspellings, in fact, tend to come from children.

Most misspellings of children and adults do not correlate with these intentional misspellings. While I try not to remember every misspelling I have encountered, the majority do not resemble the "cute" misspellings of storefronts and brand names. Southerners love their doughnuts, but I have never seen a *krispy* or a *kreme* in their writing unless it is referring to one particular doughnut chain whose name I will not mention.

In other words, most people learn early in life that misspellings can be nothing more than a cheap marketing trick — one they should not try at home or in the classroom. Actually, educational research indicates that store signs, traffic signs, and other public and practical "texts" provide children with the functional types of reading they need to make sense of written words and appreciate their real-world value. When a child vacantly stares at a cereal box at breakfast, he or she is fueling up on a little bit of literacy, as well as a lot of sugar. No doubt, it might be the golden arches of McDonald's that prompts children to salivate more than Pavlov's dog, but their brains also assimilate the word that inevitably appears with the arch. This basic process is part of how people naturally acquire a reading ability — by practical, real-life situations in which decoding written words provides the reader with benefits, such as calories and "free" plastic toys.

Being able to read a sign or label on a jacket will not by itself make a person literate. If that were the case, our advertisement-drenched nation would have 100 percent literacy. But as a whole, these incidental acts of literacy do their part in helping us learn to read, write, and even spell.

The negative impact of intentionally misspelled store signs, business logos, and brand names is slight because their context is unique compared to the writing most of us do. The misspellings we see in e-mails, instant messages (IMs), and other electronic media are much more infectious because these texts resemble (or constitute) what we ourselves write. People were misspelling long before the first e-mails and IMs crawled through telephone wires. Nonetheless, the contributions of electronic communication to our spelling problems are increasing as we are bombarded with messages thrown together with the mistaken belief that everybody forgives a few misspellings in these hastily composed texts. For some young people, "txtspk" (textspeak) is becoming almost second nature.

Technology alone is not to blame for our exposure to misspellings. Ironically, many textbooks and teachers who want to help their students spell make the problem worse. Educational research has indicated that when a teacher spends more time on incorrect rather than correct examples, all the student really remembers is how to re-create the errors (hence, in this book I try to have at least as many correct as incorrect examples of American spellings).

Doesn't our flawed spelling system explain not only why people misspell but also why we have too many illiterate people for an industrialized nation?

Our spelling system is part of both problems, but other factors contribute as well. Legions of books speculate on the causes of illiteracy, and it is beyond my scope to offer an in-depth analysis of various theories attempting to account for illiteracy. Spelling is closely associated with literacy, so I cannot ignore the topic either.

The inconsistent, illogical spellings of such words as *thorough*, *eucalyptus*, and *khaki* do not represent the spelling system as a whole. The English spelling system is, in truth, more consistent than we might assume. People often do not discern the consistencies because they usually cannot articulate the complex rules most readers internalize without even knowing they have done so.

Still, our spelling system causes hardships for many children and adults learning to read and write. The literacy rate would improve if English spelling were more straightforward, but research has proved that far more than spelling is involved in becoming literate. Even the most basic levels of literacy entail more than being a competent speller. The grammar of English—the rules for how words are put together to form sentences—is also a major factor, along with understanding the meaning of words. Spelling a word is immaterial unless a child knows the meaning of the word and how it can be used with other words to create a sentence. Even if our spelling system were simpler to learn, a person must master other skills to become literate, so we cannot assume the root cause of poor spelling, much less literacy, is a flawed spelling system.

Aren't misspellings the result of not being skilled at memorizing?

Memorization is only part of the problem and solution. Being able to memorize a sequence of letters can certainly help you spell, just as having a poor memory makes spelling more difficult. Up until the 1960s, American educators and textbooks tended to approach spelling as if it were a simple matter of rote memorization and, at times, of what they considered to be the rules. We should not nostalgically assume these ideas must have been correct because Americans "back then" were better spellers. People have been lamenting the spelling problem in America ever since we have become a nation, as evidenced by the many attempts over the years to fix the problem by changing the spelling system itself.

Memorizing is only part of what goes on when people learn to spell, so a faulty memory is not the cause of most people's misspellings. Spelling is also a problem-solving activity in which people of all ages, without always being conscious of what they are doing, test and create hypotheses about our elaborate system of spelling rules and preferences. Since the 1960s, the vast majority of research on spelling indicates that learning to spell is a sophisticated developmental process. That is, most children learning to spell go through fairly predictable but flexible stages. During this process, they draw on increasingly complex forms of logic and reasoning in order to interpret the symbols of written discourse and match these not only to sounds but to ideas and their world.

Most misspellings are not the result of a poor memory, or stupidity for that matter. With the exception of proofreading mistakes or "slips of the pen," misspellings usually result when a person, consciously or subconsciously, logically produces a spelling based on similar words or general principles. The problem, of course, is English spelling is not altogether logical or consistent.

Regardless of age, we do not memorize spelling rules as much as we internalize them as a result of cognitive processes that typically operate below the level of consciousness. Have you ever been taught, for instance, that in English *ck* can appear in the middle or end of a word, but never at the beginning? This rule, like hundreds of others you naturally acquired, is so powerful that even when people are asked to make up nonsense words, they will almost never start them with *ck*, as if it were a cultural taboo.

Some teachers, parents, and students use the terms *dyslexia* and *reading disability* far too casually, but there is no denying some people have a neurological or processing disorder that makes some aspects of literacy, usually spelling, unusually difficult. I myself have an extremely hard time spelling words "in the air"—in speech (hence, no spelling bee awards have ever adorned my mantle). Give me a pen and paper, and my orthographic prowess doubles. If spelling were only a matter of memorization, such a phenomenon would not occur. According to certain theories, in fact, the parts of the brain we do use when memorizing spellings do not correlate with portions used for other types of memorizing. While there are many unknowns in terms of language disorders and how our brains process the printed word, researchers have proved that (1) there are complex cognitive mechanisms at work and (2) memorization accounts for only part of the problems people face, and only part of the solution.

If spelling is naturally acquired as a result of everyday reading and writing, then isn't the problem simply a result of people not reading and writing enough?

Writing, reading, and spelling are so closely connected that it is easy to assume improvement in one skill means improvement in the others. However, this cherished belief, one I held myself for many years, cannot fully explain why people misspell. I will continue to encourage people to read and write as one way of improving spelling, but much more is needed for most adults to make notable gains.

The notion that spelling need not be taught directly was, in part, a result of related research that educators misinterpreted. True, people can acquire basic literacy and spelling skills from reading, including the reading of store signs as well as novels. In fact, you can acquire the basics of any skill, whether it be golf or spelling, merely by doing the activity. But if I did not have someone telling me when I am holding a golf club incorrectly, I would likely develop a poor swing that might move the ball, but not necessarily in the right direction.

Don't misunderstand me. Reading and writing can improve our spelling ability, but these acts alone are not enough to provide the help most adults need. If it were, then we would find that poor spellers have not read or written much. Too many exceptions exist to claim such is the case. Indeed, the debates continue as to the "chicken/egg" relationship between reading and spelling. Do most people learn to read by first learning how to spell, or should the focus be on reading so people will learn spelling in a more meaningful context?

Many researchers have established what most of us already know: reading, writing, and spelling are highly interrelated. Researchers, though, have also determined that the correlation is uneven and the cause/effect relationship is not straightforward at all. *Making* a person read or write, for instance, will not necessarily improve that person's spelling ability. A person can even volunteer to be a voracious reader and still not spell (or write) well. Quite likely, each day you come across words you cannot spell, yet you know what they mean when you read them. Just because you can decode words does not mean you could spell them yourself.

Are your chances of spelling a word correctly enhanced if you see it in print? The best I can say is "possibly." The different cognitive activities involved in reading and spelling mean the chances of improvement can range from practically no progress at all to mastery of the word in question. Reading and writing are especially useful in providing the means by which children naturally acquire the intuitive rules governing spelling (not to mention grammar), but most adults need assistance with issues that go beyond these fundamental rules of orthography, issues such as when and how to apply these diverse rules in particular words.

So can we prevent misspellings by studying the rules that govern the English spelling system?

The answer is, again, possibly. Undoubtedly, it would be inane to study every rule we have for spelling, such as the prohibition against beginning a word with *ck*. First, most of these rules are acquired so naturally that, even at a young age, few native speakers of English break these internalized rules. In addition, the spelling rules and tendencies number in the hundreds, if not thousands, depending on how comprehensive you want to be. Learning them all would, even for those of us enthused about spelling, be mind numbing.

Every spelling system is composed of different types and levels of rules, so we need to think carefully about what we mean by "learning the spelling rules." If we mean rules that determine the way in which letters match up to sounds, then relatively few adults need to agonize over all these possibilities. Consider, for example, the results of a study that Virginia Holmes and Anne Castles, two professors of psychology at the University of Melbourne, published in 2001. They examined the backgrounds, spelling skills, and spelling strategies of university students who were poor spellers and compared the findings to above-average spellers. Their study found that the poor spellers knew just about as much as the good spellers in terms of how letters correspond with sounds. The results indicate that, at least with adults, there is little sense in covering the fundamental rules on letter/sound relationships.

Which rules are worth learning? Certainly not the legions of fine-tuned rules, nor those covering merely the basic relationship between letters and sounds. For older teenagers and adults, only a few "rules" are worth studying. These worthwhile rules are patterns and tendencies more than firm rules, and they focus on just the major conventions that apply to certain words. I will explain these ideas in the next chapter. Studying judiciously selected rules can be one way to improve a person's spelling, but in general the study of spelling rules is vastly overrated, at least in terms of adults.

Younger children, as research shows, can be aided by an explicit discussion of rules, but these rules must also be carefully selected. Children progress through predictable stages of development, and it makes little sense to teach them a concept they are cognitively not equipped to deal with yet. For example, almost all preschoolers learn consonants far more easily than vowels, largely because consonants are easier to pronounce and distinguish in somebody else's speech. Frequently, preschoolers will spell words without even using vowels—a temporary stage and not a sign of some sort of vowel-deficit syndrome. Many teachers and parents mistakenly assume they should rush in with rules and exercises bought from Phonics "R" Us and teach vowels. That can come later, if necessary. It is better to capitalize on what young children are beginning to understand—consonants—rather than jump to the confusing realm of vowels.

Causes of Misspellings

The assumptions we've discussed are not completely incorrect, yet people have a tendency to oversimplify misspelling by reducing the causes to just one or two of these reasons. Here are more reasonable ways to express these issues:

- Because of their genetic makeup, some people might be more inclined to spell correctly than others, yet almost all people can improve their spelling skills.
- Anyone who frequently sees a misspelling is more likely to create a similar misspelling, but deliberately misspelled ads, signs, and brand names have a negligible effect.
- The complexity of our flawed spelling system is a notable source of misspellings, but it is not the only source.
- Although a poor memory will hamper a person's ability to spell, memorization accounts for only part of the mental process involved in spelling.
- Misspellings often result from a writer logically attempting to spell a word based on similar words or internalized rules governing English.
- For adults at least, most misspellings are not caused by their inability to remember rules dictating which letters can make which sounds. In fact, studying all the rules

that govern English spelling will not enhance most people's spelling.

- Although writing and reading can improve many individuals' spelling, misspellings in general do not indicate a person has failed to read and write sufficiently.

By no means is this list exhaustive in terms of why people might not understand how to spell a given word or struggle with spelling in general. Numerous physical or neurological conditions affect many adults' spelling. A hearing-impaired person, for example, will often struggle when applying the rules based on the relationship between letters and the sounds they reflect. If a person is accustomed to using only one dialect and it differs considerably from Standard English, then he or she might encounter formidable problems in spelling.

In the previous list, you might have noticed I left off one major reason why people misspell. I have done so because generally speaking it is categorically different from the others. Thus far in this chapter, I have focused on what we could call a "knowledge error"—misspellings that occur because the writer essentially does not know the correct spelling or is unable to produce it, unless by luck or chance. The problem might stem from a learning disorder, from seeing the word spelled incorrectly, from guessing the spelling of the word based on how it might be pronounced, or from any other factor that leads the writer to misunderstand how the word is spelled. Most of the time, the writer could look at this word several times and not realize it is misspelled—not until a spell-checker or reader points out the problem.

In contrast, a "proofreading mistake" is, as the name suggests, a misspelling that the writer can recognize as a misspelling and can correct *if* he or she looked at the misspelling more carefully and tried to correct it. A "knowledge misspelling" is a more fundamental problem with knowing the correct spelling. A proofreading misspelling results from not correcting a word the writer knows how to spell. Proofreading mistakes of any sort, not just misspellings, result from numerous factors, including the following:

- Being rushed, or feeling rushed, while writing
- Apathy or lethargy
- Negative attitudes about writing, the topic under discussion, or even the reader
- Reckless abandon resulting from enthusiasm or passion about the topic under discussion
- Visual problems, as in eyestrain, tiny font, or poor eyesight
- Physical difficulties (try writing and spelling correctly with a broken finger)
- Poor motor skills or hand-eye coordination
- Distractions during the writing situation, such as excessive noise or interruptions
- Typographical or keyboarding slips
- Computer-generated mistakes, as when the spell-checker errs
- Momentary memory lapse
- Fatigue, stress, anxiety
- Assuming the situation is so casual readers do not mind misspellings (sometimes a correct assumption)
- Carelessness in general

A less technical name given most of these problems is "dumb mistake," or people often just label the writer as "lazy" and "sloppy." In fact, many of us employ harsher terms to describe the misspellings we commit ourselves.

For the most part, a misspelling is either a knowledge error or a proofreading mistake, but this is not always an either/or matter. Some misspellings fall along a continuum. For instance, you might have written a word and felt the spelling just does not look right. The spelling might not seem right because English orthography is not altogether logical, or you might intuitively realize your spelling does not reflect the way you have seen the word spelled in other people's writing. In short, sometimes we are not certain if a word is spelled correctly or not. Is this a lack of knowledge? In some ways, yes—because we do not know the correct spelling. Still, these doubtful spellings are primarily a matter of proofreading, for they have not escaped our attention while rereading. Knowledge errors, as noted already, tend to be misspellings we do not detect because we think they are fine as is.

This list does not reflect all the reasons why we misspell words when we know the correct spelling. Sometimes, the reasons are not only intentional but outright devious. You might have noticed you are still e-mailed spam even though you use a filter to screen e-mails, blocking all messages that contain, say, the word *Viagra*. Spammers can get around many filters by intentionally using the misspellings *Viagrra* or *Viagera*.

At other times, a writer might intentionally misspell words just to aggravate a reader, especially by misspelling that person's name. One student I managed to annoy with a low grade on a paper suddenly seemed to become dyslexic, but strangely only with my name. In the heading of papers she turned in afterward, I became "Dr. Bison," "Dr. Beastly," and finally "Dr. Beasonofa." I never could enable her to understand that some misspellings are more detrimental than others.

Similarly, haven't "top-forty" musicians long misspelled their names and song titles as one way to annoy the establishment, in addition to using the same marketing ploy of U-Haul and Toys "R" Us? Consider song titles such as "Nothing Compares 2 U" and "Chic 'n' Stu"—or band names such as OutKast, Def

Leppard, and Limp Bizkit. To be fair, we also have the occasional tune that has a built-in spelling lesson, such as Aretha
Franklin's "R-E-S-P-E-C-T."

Those of us who are not musicians cannot so easily justify
misspellings as symbols of rage against the machinery of the
establishment. Most often, our proofreading mistakes are less
sublime problems we should have detected and corrected, even
if the spellings occur for understandable reasons.

At times, misspellings result when a writer is heavily
engaged in thinking. Linguists have shown that the more attention a person gives to *what* he or she is saying, the less attention is given to *how* it is being said. Despite the interrelatedness
between thinking and language, we can handle only so much
when writing or speaking about complex topics and difficult
problems. In writing, misspellings (as well as other mechanical
errors) easily occur when we focus on exploring new ideas or
any sort of thinking in which our brain gives the finer aspects
of writing a lower priority in order to avoid cognitive overload.
In other words, our brain cannot do everything at once, so
sometimes spelling goes on the back burner.

Will readers forgive our misspellings if, somehow, they realize our first priority was providing them with astounding ideas
and remarkable insights? Probably not. I believe such misspellings do not present a problem when they occur in a draft,
but the finished piece of writing that readers are given should
be proofread to prevent even the most noble misspellings.

Are Errors More Common than Mistakes?

To what extent do proofreading mistakes account for misspellings? My experience suggests that, since the late 1980s,
most adults' misspellings could have been prevented by proofreading. Word processing and, more specifically, spell-
checkers have changed the way America misspells.

As noted earlier in this book, spell-checkers do not catch all misspellings, but they do detect the majority. If we do not know how to spell *euthanasia, embarrass,* or *hallucinogenic,* our spell-checker will kindly correct them for us, often without our even knowing it did so. In such ways, technology saves us from producing knowledge errors. When the spell-checker is not available or not used, our true knowledge of spelling will be exhibited to any reader who can spot the misspelling. So much writing can be spell-checked that knowledge-based misspellings have become less common, providing the illusion that people's understanding of spelling is improving.

When personal computers and word processing became widespread in the early 1980s, it appeared at first that this technology was having a negative effect on spelling. In a study published in a 1992 issue of *Written Communication,* two researchers, Robert Connors and Andrea Lunsford, found evidence of this phenomenon when they compared college students' essays when handwritten, word processed without spell-checkers, and word processed with spell-checkers. In terms of the three thousand handwritten essays examined, the researchers found that using *its* for *it's* (or vice versa) was by far the most common misspelling. The *its* or *it's* misspelling was so widespread the researchers decided to grant it separate status as an error of its own, rather than lumping it in with more pedestrian misspellings.

Not surprisingly, the spell-checked papers had far fewer misspellings per number of words than the papers that were word processed but not spell-checked. The spell-checker reduced the rate of word-processed misspellings by more than half. However, the handwritten essays also had about half as many misspellings as the papers that were word processed but not spell-checked.

Although the data might be different today or with a different set of adult writers, the results suggest that word processing without spell-checking will hurt, rather than help, most writers in terms of misspellings. Why would this be? One would think that a word-processed paper, even if not spell-checked, would be easier to proofread and correct than a hand-written paper. Connors and Lunsford suggest that one answer to this puzzle is simpler than we might think: word processing produces typographical errors whereas handwriting does not. For example, spelling *living* as *livig* is almost surely not a problem related to knowledge. Almost all literate adults know how to spell *living* or would not leave out the *n* if they were to misspell this word. In a report I just examined, a student similarly meant to type *create* but mistyped it as *crate*. Because *crate* is an actual word, both he and his spell-checker did not catch the mistake. In Connors and Lunsford's study, these sorts of obvious misspellings, typographical mistakes, and homonym confusion primarily accounted for the difference between the handwritten and word-processed papers that were not spell-checked.

Because the writers of the word-processed papers had the option (or were required) to revise their drafts, we have to wonder—why did they not catch these typographical mistakes and other simple misspellings? The answer is especially important because it directly pertains to today's word processors that almost insist you use a spell-checker. The researchers propose that even obvious misspellings can be more difficult to catch because the computer screen or finished typed page makes even simple misspellings look "natural"—finished, published, and ready to be read. The clarity and professional appearance of the page can make the writer willing to assume the spellings are equally professional. Also, the ease of reading a word-processed page makes many writers read too quickly even when proofreading, especially when compared to the pace at which they read their handwritten prose. Whatever the reason, word processing can increase the number of simple mistakes we make and do not detect.

The same study also confirmed the fallibility of spell-checkers. Spell-checked papers had an average of .36 misspellings per one hundred words. The majority were homophone misspellings. With this type of error, the writer misspelled the word by using a different word that is pronounced the same way (e.g., *they're* for *their*), so the spellchecker did not catch the error because the homophone was correctly spelled. It is difficult to use this study as a basis for identifying the most commonly spell-checked words. Interestingly, only a handful of words were misspelled more than once in the one hundred spell-checked essays used in the study. Homophone errors of one sort or another, though, were extremely common.

A related type of misspelling more closely borders on being a "wrong word" error rather than a misspelling. In Connors and Lunsford's study, the writers would use these faulty spellings:

an for *and*
that for *than*
crowed for *crowded*
on for *one*
ran for *run*
women for *woman* (and vice versa)
of for *or*

Such odd misspellings are still misspellings. Like homophone errors, these misspellings involve using the wrong combination of letters in a flawed attempt to represent a word in print.

The more important point is that most "wrong word" misspellings are proofreading errors. Surely, the adult writer understands *that* is not spelled *than*. What we do not know, especially with extremely automatic spell-checkers that make changes in the blink of an eye, is whether this writer made a keyboard error by typing *than, or* whether the word processor changed a different typo by mistakenly inserting *than* instead of *that*. Either way, the writer likely knew how to spell the word but did not proofread carefully. Ultimately, the source of the mistake is not so much carelessness as our growing inclination to trust technology so we can focus on what we consider more important things. That's not a bad approach, as long as we also remember to look at the little things that matter.

At times, we cannot tell by merely looking at someone's misspellings and know if these are proofreading or knowledge errors. Consider the italicized misspellings from this essay written by a first-year college student:

- Due to this *excersise,* I can *right* a rhetorical analysis.
- It was the small cemetery off *too* the side, but everyone *new* it was there.
- The grounds are in *dyer* need of repair.
- Now I can use *then* in my next paper.
- After finishing Part A of this *excersise*, I reread my paper.

As is the case with many people, most of this writer's misspellings are proofreading accidents, which he could have easily corrected without needing to learn a new spelling at all, heaven forbid. Surely, using *right* for *write* is a proofreading mistake—a misspelling that is doubly annoying when produced in a writing course. The student also knew better than to use *new* for *knew* and *too* for *to*. These three mistakes are homonym misspellings that careful proofreading would have prevented.

Yet what of *dyer*, which should have been *dire*? Sometimes, even misspellings can help inquiring readers learn something new. I knew *dire* to be the correct choice in the sentence, yet I consulted a dictionary for *dyer*—a word not in my lexicon—just to see if it could be plausible. Apparently, this is an archaic term going back to the Middle Ages and referring, as the name suggests, to someone who dyes clothing for a living or, less obviously, to a type of grape. What we do not know is if the writer made a typographical mistake (which the spell-checker did not catch because *dyer* is a real, if antiquated, term) *or* if the writer really thinks *dyer* is the correct spelling. For most young adults, reading or writing the word *dire* is so rare they might not know the correct spelling is as simple as the word sounds. My guess is this word is likely another proofreading error based on a homonym, yet possibly the student does not know how to spell *dire*.

Finally, this student's most puzzling misspelling is *excersise*. No word is correctly spelled this way, so it is not a homonym mistake. The fact that it is misspelled twice does not prove the error is a knowledge error; I have seen many proofreading goofs appear the same way twice within one document. What seems most unusual, though, is that the paper was clearly spell-checked, yet this same misspelling appeared twice. It is a text-book example of a phonetic misspelling—misspelling a word based on how the writer might pronounce it. So why did the student not change the misspelling when any spell-checker would encourage him to do so, not once but twice? There is a remote possibility this particular misspelling was mistakenly added to the database for the student's spell-checker, but why anyone would do so is difficult to explain. Tampering with a roommate's spell-checker is a college prank only the most severe techie geek would consider.

This student's double dose of *excersise* seems odd, but it is surprisingly not so unusual after all. In the previously mentioned study, Connors and Lunsford also found that even spell-checked papers contained glaring misspellings that students decide to keep. Do these writers assume they know more than the spell-checker? Unlikely. My guess is sometimes writers have a blind spot for misspellings that look right to them, especially phonetic spellings. Even wavy red lines that spell-checkers insert under misspelled words are not enough to overcome these blind spots. Another reason, then, why spell-checkers do not always work is users do not look closely enough at the flagged misspellings, as well as not looking closely enough at errors the computer did not flag at all. I have sometimes missed not only a misspelling but a word flagged by the spell-checker. But because I know such oversights are possible, I now go through the document once looking just for red wavy lines indicating a misspelling.

Misspellings have many origins, yet other research also indicates that, with or without spell-checking, most misspellings of adults are proofreading mistakes they could have detected. To understand why these and other misspellings occur, we should again look more closely at the heart of our spelling system—the way in which it does, and does not, reflect the way we speak.

Why Spelling Is Not Alphabetic

Many people struggle with spelling because they do not consciously realize it is no longer designed to be based on speech alone. They must understand that a major operating principle of English spelling has little to do with pronunciation.

I should now be direct about a concept I have touched on elsewhere. Our spelling system is not merely alphabetic; it is also morphemic. By *alphabetic*, I refer to how letters match up with particular speech sounds. This is the way we are taught to think about spelling and writing. Because of our education and intuitive understanding of the alphabetic aspects of spelling, we yearn to spell words according to how they sound, hence the imperfect but reasonable spelling of *cat* to reflect the

<k>, short <a>, and <t> sounds we hear when we must speak of cats.

Yet we know many written words do not neatly match up so nicely with speech. Since 1066 A.D., when French infiltrated English and disturbed what had been a much simpler alphabetic system, English spelling has become progressively morphemic. By *morphemic*, I mean that our orthography is partially based on meaningful combinations of letters (morphemes). Take the word *certain*. This is essentially one morpheme, yet by adding other morphemes such as prefixes and suffixes, we create words and spellings such as *uncertain*, *certainty*, and *certainly*. In these examples, the morphemes do not disturb the way in which the letters match the sounds they typically represent. The alphabetic and morphemic aspects of English usually manage to coexist in harmony.

Consider how we take the morpheme *child* and add a morpheme to create the plural form, *children*. For historical reasons, *i* is short in *children*, long in *child*. The spellings do not utilize a silent *e* (or a similar device) to distinguish the different pronunciations of *i*, so these two words seem an easy target for critics of our spelling system. Would it make more sense to spell these as *childe* or even *chilldren*? Or spell *soften* as *sofen*, while keeping *soft* as is? Perhaps, but English spellings sometimes sacrifice the letter/sound principle so readers can more readily see the connection between words sharing a morpheme. The morphemic aspect of spelling allows us to make connections not only between words per se, but between ideas. The meaning relationship between *mental, mentality,* and *mentation* is clearer because of the visual similarities.

A morpheme can be a word ending such as *-ed*, which is our most common means of showing a verb is in the past tense. Thus, we end most past-tense verbs with *-ed* even though it can stand for different sounds, as with *treated* versus *spelled*. Once again, keeping the same *-ed* morpheme helps readers focus on the meaning they have learned to expect with that morpheme, despite the inconsistent letter/sound relationship.

In addition to helping us predict the meaning of words, morphemes assist us in spelling these words. One reason why most adults can spell tens of thousands of words is not because they memorized the sequence of letters in each word but because they memorized patterns—patterns such as those created by recurring morphemes. Once you realize the morphemes *chrono* and *chron* deal with the concept of time, you have an easier time spelling words having these morphemes. English has about a dozen common words beginning with *chrono-* (such as *chronology* and *chronoscope*), while many more incorporate *chrono* or *chron* in other positions (as with *diachronic* and *synchronize*). The pronunciation of a morpheme might vary. Compare, for example, the short <o> sound *o* makes in *chronicle* versus the <uh> it makes in *anachronism*. However, the consistency of the morpheme's spelling more than compensates for the inconsistency of how *o* is used to reflect two different vowel sounds.

As I will discuss later, knowing common root words and morphemes can assist us in spelling words we have never seen in print, a strategy commonly used by most spelling bee champions. In fact, several studies have shown that most children progress as spellers by considering the alphabetic or phonetic nature of English but then moving to an important transitional stage of understanding the morphemic aspects of English. Before students are able to spell most words correctly, they first must appreciate this morphemic aspect, yet many do not— sometimes because they did not receive sufficient direct instruction, but at other times because they were bombarded with instruction on morphemes before they were ready for this stage of learning.

We need to be cautious about our deeply rooted assumption that English spelling is truly alphabetic in the sense that each letter *must* stand for a particular sound. Our system is alphabetic in most regards, but to an important degree it is now morphemic.

Late Old English was much more alphabetic, and simpler. We need to understand, however, that this loss of simplicity is not without benefits. English has since taken tens of thousands of loanwords that have given us morphemes such as *chrono*, onto which we can add other morphemes to express and explore an array of ideas that did not greatly concern Anglo-Saxon tribes of the Dark Ages. I cannot claim that an increasingly complex orthography ushered in the Renaissance or that a flawed alphabetic system is synonymous with progress. Nonetheless, the English spelling system and its shortcomings are directly tied to the development of ideas and productive interactions among diverse cultures.

Understanding the morphemic nature of spelling provides a more accurate understanding of our spelling system, and it suggests what we might study to improve our own spelling. First, though, we should consider two other aspects of the alphabetic side of spelling: phonetic misspellings and their counterpart, also known as spelling pronunciations.

But It Sure Sounded OK When I Said It

Former vice president Dan Quayle is not the only politician whose spelling skills haunted his political career.

According to legend, Andrew Jackson, who was elected president in 1828, ushered the acronym *OK* into the American lexicon. He supposedly thought *OK* stood for "all correct," which he pronounced as "oll korrect."

Most likely, the etymology of *OK* actually goes back to the 1830s when Boston newspapers used such acronyms as a form of mockery. The misattribution to President Jackson has its origins in vicious politics of the 1820s. During the 1828 campaign, not only was Jackson accused of being an adulterer, he was even accused of being a totally incompetent speller. Both charges had some basis. Jackson did, after all, once proclaim, "It's a damn poor mind that can only think of one way to spell a word," and in 1791 he had married without realizing his new wife was legally still hitched to someone else. The press and his political rivals greatly exaggerated and fabricated aspects of Jackson's orthographic and matrimonial woes. Strangely, the adultery issue has been all but forgotten, yet Andrew Jackson is still widely considered to be, so far, the poorest presidential speller ever, with the phonetic misspelling *OK* wrongly deemed his lexical contribution.

Phonetic misspellings result when writers spell a word based on the way they *think* it is pronounced, such as spelling *elementary* as *elementry* or *prefer* as *perfer*. The term *OK* may or may not be a true phonetic misspelling, yet this simple word, with its convoluted history of half-truths and distortions of how speech and spelling relate, is a symbol of larger problems within our spelling system.

Spell-checkers detect and correct many phonetic misspellings, yet anyone who wants to be a better speller should think carefully about what is both obvious and confusing: words are not always spelled as most people might pronounce them. Given our stubborn insistence that spelling should be truly alphabetic, our misspellings—whether they are knowledge errors or proofreading mistakes—are usually related one way or another to how we assume the words are pronounced. The problem is compounded when we mispronounce words and then base the spelling on faulty pronunciations.

We each have our own way of pronouncing words, so it is difficult for me to know which ones you might pronounce "incorrectly" and how your resulting pronunciations differ from the spellings. In truth, the notion of "correct pronunciation" is nebulous, especially in dialect-rich America. For many decades, people in search of the right way to talk have turned to books such as *20,000 Words Often Mispronounced* (1889), *You Don't Say!* (1937), and *Big Book of Beastly Mispronunciations* (1999). I have no problem writing a book dealing with correct spelling. Unlike pronunciation, spelling has recognized standards for correctness within a given nation, and people are not very forgiving when other people cannot adhere to these standards. With speech, we have pronunciations in dictionaries right beside the spellings, yet most people rarely consult any dictionary for a pronunciation. Within certain boundaries, we are tolerant of most pronunciations, and "correct pronunciations" are not nearly as fixed as the spellings associated with Standard English.

Nevertheless, I admit some pronunciations are more conventional, accepted, or formal than others. Most people, for example, will maintain that *epitome* must rhyme with *me*, not *home*. I have thrown in the towel with *forte*, which historically has been pronounced much like *fort* unless used as a musical term and thus pronounced <fore-tay>. Even the most conservative dictionaries have forsaken me on that one. Many a speaker has made a gaffe by not correctly pronouncing the name of the city, state, or stadium in which the speech takes place. Soon after I moved to Spokane, Washington, I began to cringe when national newscasters and visitors pronounced the city's name with a long, rather than short, *a*. When President Bush visited Nevada in 2003, he pronounced *Nevada* as many, if not most, Americans do: <Ne-vah-da>. With the correct pronunciation (in Nevada anyway), the middle syllable rhymes with *glad*. The state's press and local Democrats did not miss this opportunity. State Senator Dina Titus noted that Bush's mispronunciation shows he does not care enough about the state to pronounce its name correctly. Of course, this president's most infamous pronunciation is <nucular> for *nuclear*, although other presidents such as Jimmy Carter (who had a degree in nuclear physics) used a similar pronunciation.

Nevertheless, determining which pronunciations are acceptable is far more subjective than determining which spellings are acceptable, especially considering how pronunciations change far more quickly than spellings do. The aforementioned book of twenty thousand mispronunciations (which seems a bit excessive to me) is outdated today given several shifts in speech, yet the spellings have remained mostly the same. Even in the present, it is difficult to say which words are most often mispronounced. One British company (Ginsters) commissioned a study once they learned most people mispronounce the company's name. Their study found that the word mispronounced most often by the British is the proper noun *Holborn*. Ironically, the word coming in second is *mispronunciation*.

Very little credible research has been conducted on the matter in America, but that does not stop people from generating list after list of mispronounced words. These lists sometimes overlap; at other times, they seem idiosyncratic or do not reflect words most average people use. The "most frequent" mispronunciations, or misspellings for that matter, often depend on the context. In my household, *caramel* tops the list, while *nuclear* must do the same at George W. Bush's. On high school and college campuses, *sophomore* has to be one of the most commonly mispronounced words. However, it rarely appears on the "top one hundred" lists of mispronunciations even though one researcher found nine different ways the word is pronounced, not even counting the three ways most dictionaries list as being acceptable:

sophmore	sothamore
sothmore	southamore
southmore	solphamore
solphmore	sopamore
sopmore	

I will not add another list of "most mispronounced words" but do want my readers to think about words having pronunciations that easily lead to misspellings. Granted, many words are challenging because their spelling does not reflect speech. The following words, however, are particularly difficult to spell because they are often mispronounced—or have an accepted pronunciation that leads to misspellings (you can leave out the <r> when pronouncing *February*, but you can't leave out *r* when spelling it). I am basing this list on American pronunciations, even though much of the English-speaking world considers all American pronunciations incorrect. To keep the focus on spelling, I provide only the correct spelling, not the pronunciations.

Commonly Misspelled Words with Troublesome Pronunciations

acumen	cholesterol	February
adultery	cinnamon	fillet
ambulance	(anti)climactic	government
Antarctic	congratulations	gyro (the food)
antecedent	controversial	height
apartheid	disastrous	hierarchy
Arctic	drivel	hundred
ask	drown	hypocrite
asterisk	electoral	integral
athlete	elementary	interest
cache	empirical	jewelry
cavalry	escalator	laboratory
centrifugal	escape	leprosy
century	especially	library
children	etcetera	literally
choleric	favorite	miniature

mischievous	prescribe	sordid
niche	prescription	succinct
nuclear	privilege	supposedly
orangutan	probably	surprise
ordnance	pronunciation	temperature
pamphlet	prospective	temporary
particular(ly)	prostate	tentative
percolate	relevant	undoubtedly
pin	repercussion	vegetable
plethora	sacrilege	wheelbarrow
prefer	sit	withdrawal
prerogative	sophomore	

My list does not capture all "difficult-to-pronounce" words that are difficult to spell. *Arctic* and *Antarctic* are just two place names (not to mention people's names) on the list, yet dozens of others are mispronounced in ways that lead to misspellings.

We could also add words that — like *pin*, *sit*, and *ask* — have ethnic or regional pronunciations that lead to misspellings. In Texas, for instance, there has been a trend for *pin* and *sit* to be pronounced <pen> and <set>, leading to homophone misspellings for some writers. I have left out most dialect-induced misspellings to focus on more "generic" or widespread difficulties, but I also believe that people tend to exaggerate the impact of dialect on adults' spelling. With very young children, such as first graders, dialect plays a more noticeable role, yet the impact on spelling decreases dramatically for most children by the time they are eight or nine. Researchers have found that regional and ethnic dialects can, at least in experimental conditions, account for some misspellings of college students, so the relationship between one's speech and spelling persists into adulthood. Still, just because a person pronounces a word differently because of a dialect does not mean a misspelling will result. Another common Texanism is to pronounce *oil* and *foil* so that they sound like *all* and *fall*. Although I lived in Texas for many years, I never once saw *oil* and *foil* misspelled in these ways. In New York City and other areas, you might hear *this* and *those* pronounced as <dis> and <dose>, yet rarely are these words misspelled either, unless a writer is trying to imitate or mock someone's speech.

The list also left off two extremely common misspellings, but I excluded them because these two words by themselves are not problematic. It is the word (or, more specifically, the sound) that comes *afterward* that brings these common misspellings into fruition. Many people misspell past-tense forms *used* and *supposed* when the next word begins with <t>. Almost always, the misspelling is followed by *to*, as seen in these examples:

She was not *suppose to* meet with me today.
I *use to* live in Florida.

Sometimes, these are proofreading mistakes the writer could easily correct. Yet I have also seen many adults who detect nothing wrong at all with these spellings, indicating a knowledge error brought about in part by the frequency of this misspelling in many people's writing. The source of the problem is that almost everyone will pronounce these misspellings exactly as they are written—by leaving out the <t> ending of *supposed* and *used* because the next word begins with the same sound. The words and sounds in *supposed to* blend together naturally, largely because of our inclination to simplify certain consonants at the end of words. Try pronouncing the final <t> in *supposed to* and you will likely create an awkward pause or annoying <t-t>.

This so-called consonant reduction occurs with other phrases and is not related to any particular dialect. Our modern term "ice cream" was originally "iced cream" before consonant reduction made "ice cream" the orthographic flavor of choice. To consider another example, try saying this sentence aloud: "Russell bought cold cuts from the store." More than likely, you pronounced "cold cuts" as <cole cuts>, leaving off the <d> sound. Few people, though, ever would misspell the phrase as "cole cuts" because there is no such word as *cole*. In contrast, the misspellings "suppose to" and "use to" contain familiar spellings, so the errors are not as glaring.

Rarely will a person misspell *supposed* or *used*—unless it appears in this particular environment, with *to* coming right afterward. Knowing this pattern helps a person avoid or catch the misspellings, but a spell-checker is of no help. For individuals prone to producing these mistakes, I have suggested that, once they believe they are finished writing, they use the "search" or "find" function on a word processor and check each instance of "use to." Automatically replacing this phrase with "used to" is not always correct, however. In this example, "use" is correct because the past tense is not needed: "I bought a container Sarah could *use to* store her toys." In contrast, "suppose to" is almost never correct.

Using the Yahoo! search engine today, I found 521,351 hits for "suppose to." On examining one hundred, I came to two conclusions: (1) not a single "suppose to" was correct on these pages, and (2) looking at these misspellings was deteriorating my own ability to spell, so I judiciously stopped.

Payback: When Spelling Affects Speech

As a final note on the uneasy relationship between spelling and pronunciation, I ask readers to consider the opposite of what they see in phonetic misspellings. In a few instances, spelling determines pronunciation, instead of the other way around. A "spelling pronunciation" occurs when people pronounce a word like it is spelled, even though a different pronunciation has traditionally been preferred.

For example, consider the long-misunderstood word *comptroller*. Around 1500, scribes who wanted *controller* to reflect its French heritage revised it to begin with *compt* (which unfortunately was not the true etymologic basis of the word, but that's another story). For centuries thereafter, *comptroller* was pronounced the same as *controller*, yet now *comptroller* is usually pronounced much as it looks, with <u><comp></u> being distinctly pronounced. This term has still not come into its own, for it rarely appears in print or speech outside of official documents, perhaps because of the uncertainty over the word's pronunciation.

When enough people use the spelling pronunciation, it can eventually become the new standard. Perhaps that partially accounts for why people can be terribly distressed when the names of their cities or states are mispronounced. They realize these mispronunciations could easily become the norm regardless of what the natives prefer. Citizens of Spokane, for instance, are well aware they are outnumbered by outsiders who have the propensity to pronounce the word as it is spelled (so *Spokane* rhymes with *cane*). Spokanites probably should not complain about outsiders appropriating the pronunciation of their city's name. An explorer's log from 1835 indicates white settlers took the name from Native Americans but should have spelled it *Spokein* to reflect the indigenous pronunciation of the word.

Among linguists who mull over spelling pronunciations, the word *often* has gained something akin to celebrity status. The word indeed has an interesting history and is a prime example of the evolving relationship between spelling and pronunciation. In early Middle English, *t* was pronounced in *often* as well as in *oft*, but during that era many words having clusters of similar consonants were simplified (or reduced) simply to make the words easier to pronounce. This is a natural trend toward efficiency and economy found in many languages. By the sixteenth century, the *t* in *often* was usually deleted in formal speech, despite the inclinations of Queen Elizabeth I to keep the sound. However, increasing literacy in America and Great Britain led people to assume the *t* should be pronounced, so the older pronunciation made a comeback. Today, most dictionaries list both pronunciations, even though many speech textbooks and self-help books put *often* on their lists of commonly mispronounced words.

Several words went through this pattern of consonant reduction. The *∂* or *t* in words such as *hand̲some*, *hand̲kerchief*, *ches̲tnut*, and even *raf̲t* were deleted long ago in speech. Yet the written word encouraged these sounds to either reappear or to be replaced by another sound (as with *∂* in *hand̲kerchief* sounding like <ng>). Not all words regained their <t> sound. It is rarely heard in *listen*, though I believe the *t* of *soften* is making a reappearance after centuries of silence, perhaps because of the influence of graphically similar *often*. Americans, more so than the British, tend to welcome these sounds back with open arms and ears.

Another pattern involves the letter *l*, which eventually became silent in many words, such as *palm, calm, almond, walk,* and *talk*. To varying degrees, the <l> sound has reemerged in these words without being considered a mispronunciation. Again, the culprit seems to be literacy. When people see the letters in print, they assume the literate thing to do is pronounce them, although everyone knows many letters are silent.

Earlier, I discussed how various changes in American speech are ongoing, with some increasing the differences among certain regions and dialects. Still, the tendency to pronounce words based on their spelling is also bringing varieties of English closer together in some regards. For example, the way Southerners pronounce *greasy* as <greazy> has been such a hallmark of their dialect that the pronunciation has been used to show the migration of Southerners to the other parts of America. Yet increasingly, young people even in the deep South prefer to pronounce the word as it is spelled, with an <s> and not <z> at the end.

I find such enunciations scandalous, but times change.

Spelling entails more than arranging letters in a particular order, or disorder if you insist on seeing it that way. Misspellings likewise involve more than failing to memorize rules or sequences of letters. The causes of misspellings are diverse and cannot be written off as mere carelessness or ignorance.

Most misspellings, at least those of adults, consist of proofreading mistakes, yet this does not mean our focus should be merely on how to scan our writing for such goofs. If I might be allowed to offer one neologism, I am convinced one factor that inhibits many people's writing is orthographobia, or fear of spelling. Even with automated spell-checkers, people often become so anxious about their own inability to spell that they avoid using or toying with new phrases and terms unless their spelling is comfortably familiar and safe.

In other words, we should not be concerned just about proofreading mistakes, but about being able to spell words that we might steer clear of because their orthography causes us anxiety. Orthographobia can stifle not only our word choice but our exploration of ideas, for words provide a foundation for ideas.

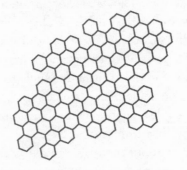

Of Rules and Fools

When I read some of the rules for speaking and writing the English language correctly . . . I think: Any fool can make a rule. And every fool will mind it.

—HENRY DAVID THOREAU (1860)

When Henry Thoreau was referring to "fools" and "rules," he was not thinking of spelling specifically, and he certainly did not always feel compelled to demonstrate his understanding of orthographic rules. Most of his writing appears in personal journals that he did not realize would be published, so it is unfair to use the many misspellings in these as evidence of Thoreau's spelling ability (though early in his writing career he felt he needed to study spelling in order to be published). He would sometimes deliberately play with spellings to make a point. Thoreau once spelled *savages* in the older form of *salvages* to emphasize its roots in the Latin word *silva*, meaning "of the woods." In referring to Native Americans of New England, he felt *salvages* more appropriately conveyed that these were, as he put it, "men of the woods"—an interpretation making the term perhaps less offensive to us today.

If my discussion of spelling has accomplished anything so far, it has shown that rules of English orthography have two defining characteristics: exasperating inconsistency that makes spelling difficult, and an open-ended flexibility that has encouraged (not just allowed) English to absorb words and ideas from around the world. A language can have this flexibility without being as confounding as English, yet our language has evolved in a way that formed an uneasy partnership between flexibility and (in)consistency.

At key points in history, we missed the spelling-reform bus, so now let's consider how we might improve our spelling skills instead of changing the entire system to fit our individual needs.

What Rules?

I often find it difficult using the words *spelling* and *rule* in the same sentence—especially because the English language as a whole lacked a formal system of rules until around the sixteenth century when the Brits decided this rustic language might be salvaged. Centuries afterward, we must consider four issues in applying the concept of "rules" to English orthography.

- English spelling has precious few absolute rules. The terms *convention* or *preference* are more appropriate, yet they fail to make the impression *rule* does when referring to guidelines that apply more often than not.
- One level of rules can be seen in the traditional "textbook rules" presented in school and self-help books. These include the familiar "*i* before *e*" rule along with a handful of other generalizations.
- Given the dearth of textbook rules that apply to most words, we also have "word-specific rules"—the dictionary rules that literally "spell out" the

orthographic rule for each word. If you want to know how to spell *onomatopoeia*, you turn to a credible dictionary for the rule, and that's that, no matter what common sense or textbook rules might suggest. The dictionary rules—as long as you do not find alternate spellings in other dictionaries.

- English spelling also has "internalized rules" that users gradually acquire, primarily through writing and reading rather than explicit instruction. These are highly specific, complex rules that make it virtually impossible for a person to misspell fish as *ghoti*, unless he or she is trying to make a statement with this deliberate misspelling.

Knowing "the rules" can help us improve spelling, but the only firm rules are the ones governing each of approximately half a million words in English. Even if you pare that down to the words the average educated adult knows, you would need to study some twenty thousand rules, at the very least.

Textbook rules are relatively few in number and usually do not assist with most spellings. One common textbook rule states that *q* should be followed by *u*. This rule almost always applies, the major exceptions being proper nouns or foreign terms such as *Iraq* and *coq au vin* (a chicken dish). A handful of other exceptions are acronyms increasingly used as words of their own (most notably, *FAQ*), along with unclassifiable peculiarities such as *qwerty* (a standard keyboard, named after the first six letters of its second row). Although this "*qu*" rule is extremely reliable, few adults misspell by forgetting to follow *q* with *u*. As with many traditional rules for spelling, the "*qu*" rule offers little help with the majority of misspelled words that plague adult writers.

What of the intuitive rules that truly govern spelling? In 1970, Richard Venezky published a landmark study of English spelling, teasing out dozens of internalized rules based on an analysis of twenty thousand words. These rules are so technical and abundant that a person might as well try learning the word-specific rules.

Fortunately, you have other options—a blend of textbook rules and internalized rules made more explicit. I will distill the most useful rules in the following pages and explain how they do and do not operate.

I Before *E*: The Legend

I will begin by considering one traditional approach to helping people of all ages spell. Until approximately 1970, spelling textbooks for schoolchildren contained, in addition to detailed lists of "spelling demons" (more on those later), numerous rules that could be applied to many words. Since that time, spelling books have placed less emphasis on such rules, although lists of individual words remain.

In both eras, most people have remembered only one rule, but it stands out among all others: *i* before *e*, except after *c*. Purists would remind us of the entire ditty:

> *I* before *e*, except after *c*
> Or when sounded as *a*
> As in *neighbor* or *weigh*.

This is a useful rhyme even if the first line is all you remember—and even if there are exceptions. A fair amount of ink has been spilled (and keyboards tapped) in failed attempts to dethrone the "*i* before *e*" rule. I assert it is worth remembering if for no other reason than it will help you avoid misspelling many words, especially these commonly used and commonly misspelled words:

receive	receives	received
receivable	receipt	conceited
ceiling	perceive	deceive
deceit	believe	believes
believed	unbelievable	believability
chief	yield	piece
grieve	thief	achieve

Except in two cases, my list does not include the various shapes these words can take if you form compounds or add prefixes and suffixes (e.g., *deceived*). I listed several forms of *receive* and *believe* because these are especially likely to be misspelled (the "*receive* words," in fact, are usually listed at the top of most people's lists of frequently misspelled words).

These words alone make "*i* before *e*" worth remembering. If you also recall the last two lines of the entire ditty, you can avoid mistakes with a few words that are sometimes misspelled, such as these terms having a long <a> sound:

deign	heir	weight
veil	heinous	sleigh
beige		

But the venerable rule is vulnerable to exceptions. Some individuals have tried to address these by adding supplementary lines to the rhyme. A fourth line that has appeared in recent years is "*Weird* and *neither* aren't the same *either*." The way some people interpret the rule, though, it would have to become an epic poem in order to include every alleged exception. First, let me list what some people consider exceptions. Although I do not believe these all contradict the rule, I will note these words because just thinking about them can provide an opportunity to master their spelling.

People frequently have listed some or all of these seventeen words as exceptions to the "*i* before *e*" rule:

weird	neither	either
height	seize	seizure
leisure	species	financier
sheik	Fahrenheit	wherein
hierarchy	fiery	codeine
stein	sovereign	

Many other words *seem* to break the rule. We will not include those having -*ing*, -*ism*, or -*ist* suffixes, such as *being* and *atheist*. Let's not include words with *pre-* and *re-* prefixes either, such as *reinvent* and *preindustrial*. That still leaves many apparent exceptions including *zeitgeist*, which seems to be a multiple offender by twice allowing *e* to arrive before *i* (though a Germanic term, it is listed in English dictionaries). Here are other supposed exceptions:

forfeit	caffeine	counterfeit
their	foreign	heifer
heist	kaleidoscope	nuclei
protein	seismic	efficient
conscientious	deficient	science
sufficient	society	friend
die	glacier	ancient
deice	albeit	forfeiture
therein		

The rule, however, actually applies to these and other words *if* we associate the phrase "*i* before *e*" not only with the letter *e* but with the *sound* of long <e>. The rule works best, in other words, when *ei* or *ie* works as one unit reflecting the <ee>

sound. Hence, the best way to present the whole rhyme is this way:

> When the sound is *ee*,
> *i* before *e*, except after *c*
> Or when sounded as *a*
> As in *neighbor* or *weigh*.

With this version, the only common exceptions are *either, neither, weird, leisure, seize, protein, codeine, caffeine, species,* and *sheik*.

Other people have tried to cover all exceptions by adding still more qualifiers to the rule, but one reason for the staying power of the simpler version is it is memorable. If the purpose is to improve our spelling rather than precisely record the nature of English, we are better off with a memorable guideline that works the vast majority of the time, as opposed to a cumbersome rule that is painstakingly accurate and utterly forgettable.

Three-Letter Words: Better than Two, Cleaner than Four

Around the world, every airport is required to have a three-letter abbreviation even if the third letter is unnecessary, as with *LAX*. For a different reason altogether, several words in English must also have three letters, even when the third has no other function than to provide a third letter.

Three-letter words might at first seem to pose few challenges to spellers, but short words can be confusing at times, especially when they have silent letters. You might benefit from remembering a guideline linguists discovered long ago:

Most "content" words in English have at least three letters.

That is, words that mean something fairly specific or concrete are rarely just one or two letters. Unfortunately, many of these words could be phonetically spelled with two letters. To avoid having just two letters, terms such as the following have either a double consonant or silent *e* added.

Extra Consonant

add	ass	egg	err
ill	inn	odd	ebb

Silent *e*

awe	bee	doe	eye
owe	see	toe	

In contrast, the majority of words having one or two letters have considerably less meaning. Usually, they are mere "function" words that do little except connect more meaningful words. Consider how slight the meaning is with *am, as, at, be, by, do, in, of, or, so,* and *to.* Function words can be three letters or more, as seen with *but* and *nevertheless.* The three-letter rule constrains *content* words, not function words.

Content words with two letters are rare—*go, ox,* and perhaps *ax* (which can be spelled *axe*). I am not alone in asserting that *I, he, it, no, my, us, we,* and even *hi* could be added to the list of two-letter content words, but others call them function terms. Either way, they are rarely misspelled.

We have never employed a three-letter sheriff who enforced this rule; it developed more or less naturally, with assistance from scribes, printers, and editors of dictionaries. Some two-letter content words might have gained their extra consonant or silent *e* for several reasons, not just conformity. In fact, nobody knows for sure why this trend ever developed. It is tempting to assume the rule arose so we would avoid more duplication than we already have. For instance, spelling *inn* as *in* would mean this two-letter spelling would have vastly different meanings. This concern is not the only origin of the three-letter rule, for it applies to only some words.

Around 1200 A.D., English developed a greater tendency to double a consonant after a vowel to indicate the vowel is short, rather than long. Some three-letter words, such as *odd* and *egg*, might have resulted from this tendency, but there is also evidence that words such as *ebb* are derived from Old English terms that predate the beginnings of the doubling trend. We might be able to figure out the logic behind the three-letter rule for airports, but the equivalent rule for content words is far more difficult to determine.

-able Enables Words

Frequently, the word endings *-able* and *-ible* sound exactly alike, so pronunciation offers little help when spelling words that have these suffixes. If you are willing to accept a "rule" that works only most of the time, remember this:

Add *-able* to a recognizable word, as with *recognizable*.

To be more precise, you add *-able* to recognizable root words. The suffix *-able*, for instance, is added to *invaluable* because of the root word *value*.

The way I suggest remembering this guideline is to associate *-able* itself with the notion of a recognizable word—by thinking of the word *able*. In this way, *-able* is connected to its fellow words.

Word + -*able*

accept + able = acceptable
adapt + able = adaptable
adore + able = adorable
agree + able = agreeable
believe + able = believable
break + able = breakable
change + able = changeable
(un)comfort + able = (un)comfortable
consider + able = considerable
desire + able = desirable
do + able = doable
exception + able = exceptionable
favor + able = favorable
impeach + able = impeachable
(im)measure + able = (im)measurable
notice + able = noticeable
pass + able = passable
person + able = personable
read + able = readable
recognize + able = recognizable
repute + able = reputable
understand + able = understandable
work + able = workable

As you can see, a word that ends in silent *e* sometimes keeps it when -*able* is attached (e.g., *changeable*), but silent *e* is more often deleted. As noted in a previous chapter, the silent *e* is kept when it signals the preceding consonant is pronounced a certain way. For instance, *e* in *changeable* indicates *g* is pronounced as <j>. (This is one of those intuitive rules we do not even realize we know.) Similarly, *e* is kept in *noticeable* so we will know to pronounce *c* as <s>.

Unfortunately, *-ible* is not so easy to peg down. Most of the time, use *-ible* when what comes before is *not* a recognizable word. Again, it might help to think of the matter this way:

-ible is not a word, so do not attach it to a word.

Look closely at what you think is a word. At first glance, *apprehens* and *permiss* might *seem* like words, but they are not.

Nonword + *-ible*

admiss + ible = admissible
apprehens + ible = apprehensible
compat + ible = compatible
comprehens + ible comprehensible
(in)cred = ible = (in)credible
ed + ible = edible
horr + ible = horrible
(il)leg + ible = (il)legible
mand + ible = mandible
neglig + ible = negligible
ostens + ible = ostensible
percept + ible = perceptible
permiss + ible = permissible
(im)plaus + ible = (im)plausible
poss + ible = possible
reprehens + ible = reprehensible
terr + ible = terrible
(in)vinc +ible = (in)vincible
vis + ible = visible

John Irving, author of *The World According to Garp*, once said he could explain to other people when to use *-able* versus *-ible* but could not apply the rule himself. This difficulty is common with many people and many spelling rules. Some conventions are hard to remember, especially when they deal with choosing between two items that sound or look alike. That is why I associate *-able* to the whole word *able* — as mnemonic trickery. People remember the "*i* before *e*" rule, which also deals with similar sounds, because a catchy rhyme is also easy to remember, and maybe dance to.

Rules for spelling are hard to remember for another reason: when we start noting all the exceptions, the simplicity of the rule dissolves, replaced by uncertainty and forgetfulness.

Not knowing the exceptions, though, can lead to problems later, not the least of which is wondering whether you can trust any rules once you feel you were misled by some. My belief is we should understand the basic rule first, and then the exceptions. Once, for example, you understand the "*-able* enables words" rule, then it is time to consider exceptions, which I will go over now if you are ready and willing to risk some confusion.

- Use *-able* with "nonwords" that end with *c* sounding like <k> (as in *amicable*, *despicable*, and *explicable*).
- Use *-ible* with words that end with *c* sounding like <s> (as in *convincible*, *forcible*, and *reducible* — all of which lost silent *e*).
- Use *-ible* with most words or nonwords that end with *-ns* (as in *defensible*, *responsible*, *sensible*. A few "*-ns* words" can, according to most dictionaries, be spelled either way (such as *condensable* or *condensible*).

The three exceptions noted here apply to only about two dozen words, but this fourth covers many others:

- Use *-able* with whole words that end in *y*, but change *y* to *i*. For instance, *rely* + *able* becomes *reliable*, not *relyable*. Other examples include *deniable*, *quantifiable*, and *variable*.

The last exception partially follows the "*-able* enables words" rule, but it does call for changing the root word's ending before *-able* is added. Elsewhere, I will discuss the "*y* to *i*" metamorphosis.

Other exceptions do not nicely fit into a category. For example, *combustible* and *deductible* are based on whole words but use *-ible* anyway; it is not a matter of their ending in *-st* or *-ct*. Additional exceptions, which tend to be *-ible* words, are as follow:

accessible	dissectible	flexible
capable	distractible	impassible
conductible	durable	impressible
destructible	exhaustible	sensible

Several dictionaries allow a few words to be spelled with either ending, such as *correctable* or *correctible*, *discussable* or *discussible*, *excludable* or *excludible*, and *includable* or *includible*.

Double Consonants and Compounds

Many people have confessed that what confuses them most about spelling is when to double consonants. These individuals of course want to know the bottom-line rule on the matter. The problem is, if there were such a rule, then people would have intuitively learned it by now and would not be making these misspellings. The truth is there are various rules governing doubling, some more reliable than others.

One type of consonant-doubling rule applies to compound words, and this particular rule is straightforward with almost no exceptions:

**Keep all letters when joining two whole words,
even if it means doubling the consonants.**

This rule applies, of course, just to single words created by putting two entire words together, as in *withhold* or *bookkeeping*. English has two and a half ways of putting whole words together: combining them completely (*copyeditor*), hyphenating them (*voice-over*), or—and this is where the "half way" comes in—splitting them into two words even though they seem to stand for one idea (*day care*, which a few dictionaries will combine).

Whether or not two words are joined is surprisingly arbitrary, as illustrated in the terms *fishhook*, *fish-eye*, and *fish fry*. My point is you should almost always double consonants in compound words when the same letter ends one part and begins the next. Following are more examples, although some have the option of being hyphenated or completely separated:

barroom	fishhook	newsstand
beachhead	glowworm	roughhouse
birddog	jackknife	screwworm
doggone	knickknack	yellowwood

Exceptions to the aforementioned rule are rare and usually deal with pronunciation. For instance, few people would pronounce both *t*'s in *pastime*, and one *e* is dropped in *wherever* because it is silent (though why *knickknack* is allowed to keep its silent *k* is another mystery).

Verbs and Double Consonants

When it comes to whether to double consonants, compound words such as the examples we've seen do not cause many spelling dilemmas. The greater problem rests with dozens of other words in which we may or may not audibly detect a doubled consonant and whether the letter is doubled regardless of what we might hear.

This problem is particularly keen when we add a suffix, especially *-ed*. A suffix is a pattern of letters attached at the end of a word. In some situations, the last consonant of the root word is doubled when a suffix is added. Rather than offer one guideline that attempts to cover all double consonants in all words, I will focus on several simpler conventions based on the type of word in question. The problem usually arises with verbs onto which a suffix is added, so I will begin with these.

Some "doubling rules" depend on whether a syllable is stressed or not, but when I begin with these, most people become more confused or just say, "Oh, OK," which usually means they are pretending to understand so I will stop talking. With multisyllable words, unfortunately, the spelling does come down to stress, but I will forestall that issue for a short while until we deal with one-syllable words.

Adding Suffixes to Verbs

1. Verbs that *already* end with a double consonant are allowed to keep it that way: *added, accessed, erred, cusses, kisses, addresses, guesses, purrs, buzzing, huffing, puffing.*
2. One-syllable verbs having a *short* vowel will normally have their final consonant doubled, unless the suffix begins with a consonant (such as *-s*): *batted, fatten, rammed, spammed, bitten, smitten, brimming, flossing, getting.*
3. Conversely, if a one-syllable verb has a *long* vowel, do *not* double the consonant after all: *bloated, hiked, snored, lured, broken, biking, biting, boring, gloating, using.* (When the consonant is not doubled, readers know to pronounce the word with a long vowel, so there is a reason behind the apparent madness.)

It's time to pause and note a few exceptions before proceeding to Rules 4 and 5. First, the few verbs that end in *x* never

have this letter doubled in a "normal" word. Anybody can pronounce *XXX-rated* by thrice saying the name of the letter, but
try actually pronouncing just two *x*'s, much less trying to say
them in a misspelling such as *boxxes*. A double dose of *x*
appears in only a few proper nouns such as *Exxon* or *John Paul
XXIII*.

Far more common are exceptions to Rule 2, with the third
rule being largely reliable. Double consonants have long been
used to indicate a short vowel, thanks in great part to the
lengthy poem by the monk Orm. However, the rule has never
been ironclad. Some exceptions are words in which *two* letters
together create the sound of one short vowel (*looking*, *heading*,
booked, *beheaded*). Other common exceptions are one-syllable
words with a short vowel but ending with *two* consonants. For
instance, *punt* ends with *n* and *t*, so *t* is not doubled (*punted*).
Also, a "short vowel" word that ends with silent *e* normally does
not have its final consonant doubled (*come* becomes *coming*, *dance*
becomes *dancing*, and *lunge* becomes *lunging*). Such words are
relatively rare.

The next two rules deal with verbs having more than one
syllable, of which there are plenty. American spellings are less
likely to double consonants than their U.K. equivalents (the
British are especially prone to double the letter *l* when given
the chance). Still, both systems have their share of consonant
doubling in multisyllable words.

4. If the verb has more than one syllable, double the
   consonant if the *last* syllable before the suffix is stressed:
   allotted, *conferred*, *occurring*, *rebelling*, *submitting*.
5. If the stress is on a syllable other than the last one before
   the suffix, the consonant is not doubled: *happened*, *focused*,
   pardoned, *visiting*, *developing*.

Most dictionaries accept single or double consonants with some words, such as *worshiped* or *worshipped*. My suggestion is to adhere to Rules 4 and 5 even in these cases (hence, *worshiped*), if for no other reason than to internalize these two conventions. My way of remembering these two rules is to remember just one. If you know Rule 4, then the fifth is a natural extension.

I learned Rule 4 by associating what I think of as the "strength" of what we see and hear in words such as *rebelling*. A double consonant, in my way of thinking, is strong—a great presence in this example of the letter *l*. This strength is reinforced by the immediate presence of a stressed syllable: *-bel'* in *rebel*. Strength goes with strength, so a stressed syllable goes with a double consonant, as in *rebelling*.

If the stress is not on the final consonant of a verb, such as *focus* (*fo'-cus*), then we would not have the strength/strength sequence (hence, *focused*).

As much as I enjoy studying rules of language, I admit to resorting to such mnemonic tomfoolery. Needless to say, develop your own if mine seem too weird. It all depends on what types of associations work best for you.

When Doubling Is Not an Option

Some spellers start seeing double too often. The complexity of double consonants in verbs seems to lure people into sprinkling extra consonants around other word endings. Fortunately, one rule will help avoid much of this unnecessary doubling:

**Never add an extra consonant when the
suffix begins with a consonant, such as *-ment*.**

Previously, I discussed *-ed* and other suffixes that begin with a vowel, but other suffixes are more straightforward. We make the issue more complicated than it is when we try to apply those rules to other suffixes. Following are examples of the simpler rule when applied to a few of the many suffixes in English. Note how these word endings do *not* result in a doubling, except when the root word and suffix just happen to end and start with the same letter (as in *embalmment*). The base words in my examples are often, but not always, verbs forms.

Word + Consonant Suffix = No Extra Letters

help + ful = helpful
peace + ful = peaceful
thank + ful = thankful

child + less = childless
soul + less = soulless
thought + less = thoughtless

careful + ly = carefully
final + ly = finally
great + ly = greatly
slow + ly = slowly

abandon + ment = abandonment
commit + ment = commitment
content + ment = contentment
defer + ment = deferment
impair + ment = impairment
reenact + ment = reenactment

aloof + ness = aloofness
sad + ness = sadness
same + ness = sameness

Note: I added extra words for the *-ment* suffix because it seems to inspire more misspellings than other suffixes.

Suffixes and the Shape-Shifting *Y*

The letter *y* can become *i* when particular suffixes are added. The rule is confusing when explained in regular sentence fashion, so I offer these visual "formulas":

Consonant + *y* + Most Suffixes = Change *y* to *i*

angry + ness = angriness
beauty + ful = beautiful
body + less = bodiless
bossy + ness = bossiness
bury + es = buries
dignify + ed = dignified
flabby + er = flabbier
happy + ly = happily
lucky + er = luckier
marry + es = marries
penny + less = penniless

y + *-ing* Suffix = *y* Does Not Change

bury + ing = burying
dignify + ing = dignifying
marry + ing = marrying

The *-ing* caveat prevents the awkward appearance of two *i*'s. We invoked what I call the "It Just Looks Funny" rule. Without this restriction, we would have spellings such as *buriing*, which looks "funny" because *ii* appears in only a handful of terms such as *coniine*, *radii*, and *Hawaii*.

Even with the *-ing* qualifier, "*y* spellings" would be simple if it were not for the fact that, as my first formula suggests, there is a different rule when a *vowel* rather than a consonant comes right before *y*.

Vowel + *y* + Suffix = *y* Does Not Change

annoy + ance = annoyance
buy + s = buys
convey + ed = conveyed
coy + ness = coyness
deploy + ing = deploying
destroy + s = destroys
enjoy + ed = enjoyed
joy + less = joyless
ray + less = rayless
replay + ed = replayed
toy + ing = toying

You can better remember this last rule if you see a pattern. Compare the sound made by *y* in these last examples with those provided with the first two equations. In the first two sets, *y* alone creates a vowel sound, such as the long <e> heard in <bodi>. In contrast, when *y* comes after a vowel, the two letters (vowel + *y*) together create one sound, such as the long <a> sound in *ray*.

These three rules describe the spellings of almost all "*y* words" to which a suffix is added. Only a few commonly used words do not follow these rules, including *ladylike*, *laid*, and *daily*.

Prefixes and Double Consonants

Verbs, along with other parts of speech, can have letters added to the front as well as the end, as seen in *reinstate* or *pretreatment*.

If added at the beginning of a word, these letters are prefixes. For adult spellers, the most common trouble with prefixes occurs when they end with the same letter that the root word begins with, as seen with *unnecessary* and *irrelevant*.

Fortunately, the rule is simple. You treat all prefixes and words the same, regardless of how the prefix starts and the base word begins.

Add the complete prefix to the complete root word, even if it means doubling a consonant.

Of course, the rule depends on your knowing what the complete prefix and root word are. Just to clarify the rule itself, though, I will focus on common prefixes combined with roots that could stand alone as complete words. This next list shows how the rule results in double consonants.

Prefix + Word = Keep All Letters

dis + service = disservice
dis + solve = dissolve
dis + symmetry = dissymmetry

il + legal = illegal
il + liberal = illiberal
il + literate = illiterate
il + logical = illogical

im + material = immaterial
im + mature = immature
im + measurable = immeasurable

ir + radiate = irradiate
ir + rational = irrational
ir + regular = irregular

mis + spell = misspell
mis + state = misstate
mis + step = misstep

non + negotiable = nonnegotiable
non + nuclear = nonnuclear

re + elect = reelect
re + enact = reenact
re + enter = reenter

un + natural = unnatural
un + necessary = unnecessary
un + needed = unneeded
un + nerve = unnerve

Do Word Lists Improve Spelling?

One traditional approach to teaching spelling involves lists of words students are supposed to study, memorize, and be quizzed over. Research is mixed as to the value of this method, especially in terms of how long students remember the spellings after the quiz, but retention is a problem with virtually every academic subject. Undoubtedly, many people do benefit from studying all sorts of spelling lists, not just lists of words. The key is they must study—not just stare at—these lists.

Let me be clear: studying word lists can help adults improve their spelling. Virtually all spelling bee champions use this strategy, but it is not the only approach they use. A great deal depends on *how* a person studies word lists. Other "listable" aspects of language besides words are also worth learning. As noted earlier, we learn to read and spell by understanding how words are composed of morphemes—meaningful combinations of letters. For instance, *reinvented* has three morphemes: *re-*

(meaning "do again"), *invent* (to devise), and *-ed* (which puts the verb in past tense). Most children come to realize that pronunciation alone will not tell them how to spell; they must also learn the morphemic nature of spelling. As we mature, we increasingly use strategies based on morphemes and other aspects of spelling that go beyond just memorizing individual letters.

Relatively few adults, in fact, improve their spelling by studying letter/sound relationships of English. Most adult spellers draw on the morphemic nature of spelling by considering how morphemes and spelling rules are applied to specific words. The vast majority of research on spelling has focused on children. Still, studies indicate at least one major reason why some adults spell much better than others do: namely, better spellers not only know spelling rules and morphemes, but they are also more likely to know *which* rules to apply to specific words. Better spellers make these choices by considering the whole word, or even how the word is used in the sentence, rather than proceeding one letter or sound at a time.

In other words, proficient spellers know which rules to apply or not apply because they avoid making overgeneralizations about rules—especially rules dealing with pronunciation and letter/sound relationships. Researchers refer to such skills as being word-specific and contextual, rather than basing spelling decisions on sweeping generalizations.

An adult should actively study a combination of factors involved in spelling. Consciously studying words is useful because it helps a person consider the word-specific nature of spelling, yet this person should also consider the general rules and basic morphemes of English to understand when and how these might apply to individual words. While memorizing the spelling of each individual word in English is impractical, spellers cannot rely on general rules alone, for these are sometimes inconsistently applied to individual words. The best spellers are more likely to think about these issues deliberately and overtly. Passively reading lists of words or rules is not enough.

Whether studying somebody else's word list or selecting a word here and there from your own reading and writing, some learning strategies are more effective than others. Sure, just writing or saying the spelling over and over again will help, but other approaches can have a more lasting effect. In Chapter 3, I made a reference to spelling becoming a "contact sport." I am not referring to the intriguing possibilities of punishing someone for a wrong spelling by means of an electrical shock or body blow. This metaphor actually has some logic about it. We tend to learn anything more from active engagement—from being physically involved one way or another.

For decades, educators and spelling entrepreneurs have suggested more socially acceptable ways of getting a person physically as well as mentally involved in spelling. They have offered different models, some so elaborate that they are unfeasible. Here, I have distilled the core ideas that work best and added a couple of twists I have found to work with adult spellers.

Five Steps for Learning a Spelling

1. **Speak:** Say the word aloud, speaking as normally as possible. Also, say it in a sentence if you have any idea of its meaning.
2. **Pronounce:** Still focusing on the printed word, say it aloud, pronouncing each letter *distinctly* unless it is silent.
3. **Analyze:** Look at the word for any morphemes you recognize—prefixes, suffixes, or root words. Say and then spell these morphemes aloud.

4. **Recall:** Now, without looking at the word, say and spell it aloud. Form a visual image of the spelling as you do so.
5. **Write:** Even if you spelled the word correctly, write it correctly at least three times without looking at the word.

When unable to spell the word correctly, repeat each step as needed. These five steps draw on various senses and activities—visually reading the word, speaking (and hearing), dividing the word into parts as well as considering the whole, recalling, and the motor skills of writing. Each complements and reinforces the others.

The steps are fairly self-explanatory, but that will not prevent me from elaborating. In Step 1 in particular, repetition is encouraged; say the word aloud a few times. In Step 2, proceed slowly. Focus on "overarticulating" the word by being especially crisp and pronouncing each individual sound, even if doing so seems unnatural.

In Step 3, being 100 percent correct in recognizing a morpheme is not essential; equally important as recognizing morphemes is actively analyzing the word, closely examining its parts as well as the whole. Still, avoid claiming there is a morpheme unless its meaning is relevant to the entire word. For example, *grammar* does *not* comprise two morphemes *gram* and *ar*. The word is only one morpheme because it cannot be divided into smaller segments that work together. In contrast, the word *professor* has two morphemes: *profess* plus the *-or* suffix.

Step 4 is particularly important. A few theories indicate that the best spellers store a "visual image" of words or are able to create a vivid visual image as they spell. In fact, if you watch the televised National Spelling Bee, you will occasionally see contestants seeming to draw the word in the air, enhancing their visual image of the word that is not there. (Perhaps ESPN

announcers will one day use on-screen special effects to draw
these words for viewers, the way they do when analyzing a
football game.)

The fifth step is, unfortunately, the only step for some people—the mind-numbing repetition of writing the word over and
over. We can learn to spell this way, yet for most of us it is a
weak strategy compared to more robust forms of learning. In
fact, there comes a point when repeating a word over and over
(in writing or speech) reduces the word to meaningless figures
and sounds—no meaning at all.

Spelling Tricks and Lists

Teachers have long suggested using mnemonic tricks to remember spellings, and these can be used with the five steps noted
earlier. Most of these devices rely on your making a semilogi-
cal connection between letters and meaning (preferably, the
meaning of the word in question). Normally, the connections
make sense only because of coincidence, rather than historical
or etymological reasons. Here, for instance, are a few common
ways to remember the spelling of troublesome words:

- **ballistic:** Ballistics deal with projectiles, and a ball is
  certainly one (<u>ball</u>-istic). The origin of the word, though,
  is not based on *ball*.
- **capitol:** The common meaning of this term (as opposed
  to *capital*) is the actual building in which a government
  might meet. Associate the *o* of *capitol* with the round
  dome of the capitol building in Washington, DC.
- **February:** This is a cold month for most people, and the
  cold makes us say, "Br." You can see *br* in *Feb<u>ru</u>ary*.
- **piece:** To distinguish this word from *peace*, remember,
  "Have a <u>pie</u>ce of <u>pie</u>."

- **principal:** To distinguish this word from *principle*, many schoolchildren have enjoyed finding an irony within this mnemonic: "The princip<u>al</u> is my <u>pal</u>."
- **secretary:** "The <u>secret</u>ary can keep a <u>secret</u>."
- **separate:** People often misspell the middle part of the word, so remember it has "a rat" (sep + <u>a rat</u> + e).

The problem with these associations is that what might work for one person can be a real stretch for someone else, which is why you should make up your own mnemonics for just those words whose spellings plague you.

Years ago, I developed a way to help me with words I would misspell even though I knew better: *it's/its* and *affect/effect*. With the latter, I learned to associate *a* in *affect* with *alter*, for these two words (*affect* and *alter*) are usually synonymous. With *it's*, I visually associate the apostrophe (') with the dot above *i*. I would envision *i* in place of the apostrophe—which correctly spells out the contraction ("it is"). As sensible as these two mnemonics still are for me, they seem to work with perhaps half of the people to whom I have generously shared my tricks of the trade. Because these tactics rely on quasi-rational associations and allusions, mnemonics work best when they reflect the particular connections each individual might be able to see between spellings and meaning.

Let us now consider specific lists of words (and parts of words) that could be studied using my five steps or a similar technique. Even outside of school, the world abounds with word lists intended to help people improve their spelling. These lists might be based on the most annoying misspellings, most-often misspelled words, "words every high school student should be able to spell," or even the most common words appearing in "Dear Abby" letters. (Perhaps not surprisingly, the pronoun *I* was overwhelmingly the most frequently used word in these letters, while the most common nouns were *daughter, friend*, and *gift*. I leave it to my readers to speculate on what these results suggest, if anything, about society or the subculture of advice columns.)

Perhaps the best-known and least-loved lists contain so-called spelling demons that terrorize the populace with impossibly erratic orthography. It is not known how the phrase "spelling demon" developed or why, but some educators of the early twentieth century made it clear that spelling was a moral matter and that these demonic words hindered schoolchildren as they traveled a righteous path toward correct spelling. The phrase "spelling demon" certainly echoes the probable origin of the word *spelling*, which is etymologically related to *spell* in the sense of "witch's spell."

Perhaps what is most frightening about these demons is they pretend to be our friends. Few lists of spelling demons include esoteric words such as *psychohistory* or *chlorosis*. No, the demons are words we might encounter each day on the streets or from the mouths of friends and family. We should not be surprised *possession* can be demonic, but even *mother* and *baptize* can appear in the same list of demons.

The people who devise lists of spelling demons do not agree on which words are most difficult, but here are words that make frequent appearances as demons. The list does not include homophones; you can assume practically every homophone that exists is a spelling demon (see my homophone list in Chapter 2).

Fifty Common Spelling Demons

apologize	harass	receive
arithmetic	height	recommend
athlete	heroes	referring
becoming	interest(ing)	restaurant
beginning	leisure	rhythm

believe	marriage	sandwich
building	mischievous	secretary
calendar	mother	separate
changeable	occasion	through
coming	occurrence	truly
embarrass(ment)	parallel	until
existence	pastime	villain
familiar	potato	Wednesday
February	privilege	women
foreign	probably	writing
grammar	professor	yield
handkerchief	rebellion	

Another list is worth studying: a listing of common morphemes. One such list focuses on major prefixes or suffixes in English:

Common Prefixes in English

PREFIX	TYPICAL MEANING	EXAMPLES
a-	without a quality	atypical, amoral
ante-	before	antebellum, antechamber
anti-, ant-	opposite, against	antacid, antigravity
bi-	two	biannual, bicep
bio-	dealing with life or biology	biosphere, biochemistry
co-	together, jointly	coauthor, coexist
con-	together, jointly	concurrence, conform
de-	remove, reduce	declassify, deodorize
dis-	reverse, opposite	disinterested, disinherit
en-	put into, cause	endear, encode
ex-	former	ex-president, excommunicate
geo-	dealing with Earth or geography	geography, geometrics

PREFIX	TYPICAL MEANING	EXAMPLES
il-, in-, im-, ir-	not, opposite of	illegible, inadequate, impossible, irrational
inter-	between, among	interagency, interconnect
intra-	within	intrastate, intranet
mini-	miniature	miniskirt, miniseries
mis-	bad	misfire, miscalculate
mono-	one	monorail, monosyllabic
multi-	many	multicolored, multifaceted
non-	not	nonsmoker, nonsense
post-	after, behind	postpartum, posthumous
pre-	before	predate, prepay
re-	do again or over	rekindle, repopulate
semi-	half, partial, twice	semicircle, semiconscious
sub-	under, lowly	subbasement, subspecies
tele-	over a distance	telephone, telecommunications
trans-	across, through	transcontinental, transpolar
tri-	three, thrice	triangular

Common Suffixes in English

SUFFIX	TYPICAL MEANING	EXAMPLES
-able, -ible	capable or worthy of something	believable, visible
-age	condition or amount	blockage, footage
-ance	state of being or action	appearance, surveillance
-ancy	condition or quality	buoyancy, pregnancy
-ant	person or thing who performs an action, state of being	assistant, deodorant

SUFFIX	TYPICAL MEANING	EXAMPLES
-ation, -ion	action or result of action, condition	strangulation, indention
-cide	killer, act of killing	suicide, ecocide
-dom	condition, domain	stardom, freedom
-ee	one who receives action (or sometimes, performs)	advisee, amputee
-ence, -ency	condition or action	dependence, complacency
-ent	one who performs action, state of being	absorbent, student
-er, -or	one or something who performs action, one who is a resident of	swimmer, actor
-esque	in the style of, resembling	statuesque, Lincolnesque
-ful	full of, resembling	wonderful, masterful
-ian	relating to	comedian, vegetarian
-ify	to make or cause	falsify
-ish	relating to, somewhat	yellowish, waspish
-ist	one who does, expert in, believes in	biologist, activist
-ise, -ize	to cause, treat, or perform	agonize, exercise
-ive	having a quality, sometimes associated with an action	effective, legislative
-less	without	meatless, spineless
-oid	having a quality, resembling	humanoid, factoid
-ology	study of	theology, psychology
-ous	having a quality	humorous, poisonous

SUFFIX	TYPICAL MEANING	EXAMPLES
-philia	tendency toward, unusual attraction	hemophilia, necrophilia
-ward, -wards	in a direction	frontward, downwards
-wise	in a certain manner or direction	clockwise, crosswise

You cannot always construct meaning by formulaically adding "prefix meaning" + "root word meaning" + "suffix meaning." Often a preffix or suffix can have more than one meaning, and sometimes the meaning of the whole word is only inferred by its parts. For instance, the prefix *homo-* as derived from Greek refers to sameness (*homophone*), but *homo* as derived from Latin refers to human beings (*Homo sapiens*). The word *autocross* does not refer to crossing oneself but to a type of automobile contest.

Nonetheless, suffixes and prefixes have customary meanings that can help you determine the spelling as well as the definition of a term. Knowing the general meaning of morphemes will help a speller recognize combinations of letters that routinely appear at the beginning and ending of words.

Prefixes and suffixes are just two categories of morphemes. By far, the most common type of morphemes involve the base or root words to which we can add prefixes and suffixes. The previous lists tend to use examples in which suffixes or prefixes are added to what is essentially already a whole word—to what linguists call a "free morpheme." For example *-ous* can be added to the word (or free morpheme) *humor*. A bound morpheme, in contrast, is not used unless prefixes, suffixes, or other morphemes are added. The suffix *-philia* is, for example, added to the morpheme *hemo*, which means "blood," even though *hemo* is not a word by itself. As with many free morphemes, *hemo* can be traced back to a Greek or Latin origin (the word *morpheme* itself has a Greek origin). For hundreds of years, English has borrowed heavily on classical languages and created new meanings by adding diverse prefixes and suffixes.

While it would be unrealistic to study every root word in English, you can improve your spelling by becoming more familiar with some. The classical morphemes are a good place to start, so the following table shows several common or useful morphemes associated with Greek or Latin. Some, such as *verb*, are not limited to being bound morphemes but can also serve as whole words, suffixes, or prefixes.

Greek and Latin Morphemes

MORPHEME	MEANING	EXAMPLES
anim	mind, feelings, soul, life	animal, animosity
ann, annu	year	annual, anniversary
bene	well, good	benevolent, benefit
chron	time	chronicle, chronic
cycl	circle, wheel	cyclic, cyclone
dic, dict	to say, dealing with words	dictate, dictionary
equ	equal	equidistant, equilibrium
ferv	to heat, boil, or bubble	effervescence, fervent
fin	end, limit	finite, definitely
fort	strength	fortify, comfort
graph	writing, drawing	graphic, calligraphy
jur	to swear	jury, perjure
magn	great	magnify, magnanimous
mut	to change	mutate, commute
ordin	order, regular	ordinary, coordinate
part	part, share	impart, particle
path	to feel, suffer	pathos, empathize
plac	to please, appease, calm	placate, placebo

MORPHEME	MEANING	EXAMPLES
pod	foot	tripod, podium
psych	mind, body, soul	psychiatry, psychotic
pyr	fire	pyromaniac, pyrotechnics
rog	to ask, propose	surrogate, interrogate
son	sound	sonic, resonant
soph	wise	philosophy, sophisticated
top	place, commonplace	topographic, utopia
val	to be strong, to be worth	valor, equivalent

With many English words, we can scarcely detect their Greek or Latin roots, despite the efforts of scribes and others who attempted to make these origins more apparent in the spellings of late Middle English and early Modern English. The word *supple*, for instance, is most likely derived from Latin *placure* (to appease), which later became *supplacos* (humbly pleading) before working its way into English by way of French around 1300 A.D. Though the *plac* root word is no longer visible in *supple*, this word comes from the same linguistic cloth as *placate* and *placid*.

Etymology, the study of word origins, can provide clues about a word's spelling and meaning, but the aspiring etymologist must be aware of the chief job hazard: what many linguists refer to as "folk etymology," or a flawed attempt to use common sense to determine word origins. The problem is that sometimes the letters or pronunciation of a word only looks like a particular root word, when in fact the similarities are coincidental. The problem is compounded when the incorrect explanation actually seems to make sense. For example, *tango* looks like the Latin root word *tang*, which means "to touch." Even people like me who are incapable of dancing a tango (or the hokey-pokey, for that mater) fully realize this dance entails an extensive amount of passionate touching. As appealing as this etymological theory might seem, it is wrong. The word *tango* has its roots in the Niger-Congo term *tamgu* (to dance), not in any Latin term.

Sometimes, the folk etymology is so compelling it causes a word to change spelling, pronunciation, and even meaning. The term *hangnail* is one of the best-known examples. The word derives from *agnail*, which originally referred to various types of skin protrusions. It has been pronounced in different ways since its development from Old English, but during the Middle English period it was much as it appears: <ag-nail>. However, when people during the early Modern English period perceived it might have something to do with a "hanging fingernail," they tended to pronounce it as <hangnail>, and *agnail* slowly deferred to this spelling.

At other times, a commonsensical etymology can stumble onto something akin to the truth. For instance, a few of my students have suggested *sonar*, like *sonic*, derives from the Latin morpheme *son* (sound). This is not quite accurate, for *sonar* is but an acronym for "sound navigation ranging." However, *sonar* owes its first two letters to *sound* (which comes from Latin *son*), so my students' etymological theory managed to explain part of the heritage of this word.

The errors you might make about a word's origin are worth committing as long as you are engaged in analyzing words, spellings, and meanings. Still, you might be careful about broadcasting your guesses about a word's etymology until you check with a trustworthy dictionary, most notably the *Oxford English Dictionary*.

Achy-Breaky Misspellings

Many critics along with embarrassed ex-fans have rated Billy Ray Cyrus's "Achy Breaky Heart" as the worst song ever. How bad is "Achy Breaky"? So bad that any singer, no matter how accomplished or inebriated, will lose all credibility immediately upon singing even the opening ten words, "You can tell the world you never was my girl."

Some misspellings have this achy-breaky effect. Most people don't like to talk about the matter, though. It is easy to condemn Cyrus's hit because we know we will be able to keep ourselves from singing it, but once we start condemning certain misspellings in the same way, we have to be forever careful that they do not creep into our own prose.

As noted earlier, there are many word lists designed to help students master or avoid certain spellings, but I have noticed something missing. Understandably, these lists focus on difficult-to-spell words or most commonly used words. What seems missing is a more delicate matter—misspellings that, to put it nicely, can really make the writer look a bit silly, as if he or she had just hammered out the first lines of "Achy Breaky Heart." Sometimes, even one misspelling can jump out at readers and make them wonder what kind of person produced this writing. I will refer to these as "egregious" mistakes—misspellings that seriously jeopardize the adult writer's credibility. Noah Webster seemed to recognize this basic problem. When defining orthography, he provided this definition and sample sentence, "Orthography: the manner of forming words with letters. Bad spelling is disreputable to a gentleman."

The issue indeed is that a single misspelling can jeopardize one's reputation, not just simply be annoying. Spelling *the* as *teh* or *two* as *too* can irritate the reader, but these goofs are not scandalous. Other misspellings elicit a far crankier reaction from the typical reader. Many of us have produced at least some of these errors, and certainly what counts as an egregious misspelling will depend on who is doing the reading and writing. Still, all spellers should consider, with a sense of humor perhaps, this idea—the notion that some misspellings will endanger our credibility far much more than others.

I submit the following list, proceeding from least to most egregious, in hopes readers will develop their own compilations and avoid such misspellings in their writing. All examples are based on actual writing; the correct spelling is in boldface for emphasis.

Misspellings That Make You Go, "Hmmmm"

- *yawl* for **y'all**: "I realize yawl have likely not eaten at this restaurant."
- *writting* for **writing**, especially when the writer claims to excel at it: "Writting is something I have always been good at doing."
- *Warshington* for **Washington**: "Last summer, a massive rally was held in Warshington, DC."
- *grammer* for **grammar**: "Employees need to have excellent grammer skills if they want to work with our company."
- *naturely* for **naturally**: "Naturely, we will have to meet in private to discuss this matter."
- the name of any city or state in which you and your readers reside: "Having lived in Louizziana most of my life, I am more than familiar with its history and culture."
- *testes* for **tests**: "Taking testes has always been difficult for me."
- *collage* for **college**: "I hope to finish collage in just three years."
- *skool* for **school**: "In high skool, I made all A's and B's except in algebra."
- *mispell* for **misspell**: "I rarely mispell."

The context can make a difference with these spellings. I am moderately forgiving when someone outside the South spells *y'all* as *yawl*. On the other hand, the eighth error in the list becomes especially distressing to read in academic writing. As I inform my college seniors, I see no reason to pass a student who is scheduled to receive a college degree yet cannot spell *college*.

My brother was once invited to a neighborhood barbeque, a friendly get-together attended by people from all walks of life. He met a bulky fellow named Paul, who was a member of a motorcycle club not known for its community service. On his arm, he had a tattoo of a motorcycle with the word "Moter" under it. My brother asked Paul if perhaps this was supposed to have said "Mother" or "Motor." Paul mumbled a derogatory remark about a tattoo artist. When my brother persisted and asked what became of this tattoo artist, Paul with a slight grin said, "If I were you, I'd stop asking questions and just eat your barbeque."

I think we can assume misspelling *any* word within a tattoo is an egregious error worth avoiding.

For adults, improving spelling means attacking the problem through several strategies, such as studying major rules and conventions, analyzing diverse types of word lists, considering etymology, being familiar with morphemes having predictable spellings, and—perhaps most important—proactively studying spelling whether it means using the five steps I suggest or other techniques that force us to do more than just "think about" the correct spelling. Because of research that indicates adults' misspellings are usually proofreading mistakes, you can likely prevent most misspellings simply by proofreading more carefully, although I hope people will be just as interested in improving their spelling skills as in avoiding spelling goofs.

Unquestionably, merely reading and writing can help improve your spelling abilities, but for most of us, passively engaging in these acts is not enough. This leads me to two final yet noteworthy suggestions, one specific and the other general.

First, when writing on a word processor, by all means use a spell-checker—but please turn off *all* automatic corrections for spelling, if not grammar. When the word processor automatically fixes misspellings, you have virtually no chance of learning from mistakes or errors. Automatic changes can occur too quickly for you to detect what you did wrong—or even know a misspelling occurred at all, given the speed at which the computer makes a switch. In addition, the quicker the computer makes a change, the more likely you will not notice if it created a homophone error, such as using *too* when *two* is what you intended.

Spell-checkers can offer a learning moment *if* you take time to understand which word you misspelled, how you misspelled it, and how it might be corrected. Apparently, some companies that produce word-processing software want us to become dependent on their product. With most versions of Microsoft Word, users have to deselect the right combination of two, three, or sometimes four options hidden under "Tools" and "Format" menus in order to set the spell-checker so users can learn to be less dependent on the machine. Ideally, the spell-checker should flag each misspelling while you are typing—but without any autocorrection. Even if all you do is right-click on the flagged word and select the appropriate choice given to you by the computer, you have made an active decision that can improve your spelling skills.

My second suggestion is not as specific but ultimately more significant because, as a principle rather than a method, it applies more often to your literacy experiences. Many years ago, I read a simple piece of advice by the educator Frank Smith. He said that, to improve our writing, we should not merely read but "read like a writer." That is, we should deliberately look at what we are reading and consider *how* it is written, by looking at sentence structure and word choice, for example. I similarly suggest we should occasionally "read like spellers." We should slow down and consider some of the spellings we encounter—the arrangement of letters, the morphemes, how a given spelling compares to similar or dissimilar words, the possible etymology, or the reason why the spelling seems to work even if it first appears illogical or inconsistent. To improve our spelling, we must take it upon ourselves to make "thinking about spellings" a habit.

Clearly, we cannot ponder the spelling of each and every word we encounter. That way lies madness.

But can we not take even a few minutes a day to look closely at some spellings found in something we might be reading, even if all we do is determine if we could produce these spellings (with eyes closed, of course)? What it means to "read like a speller" will depend on each individual, but ultimately this principle calls for a more studied, unhurried approach to at least some of our reading. In so doing, maybe we will be able to reclaim the joy of reading too often lost amidst our hectic, multitasking lives.

Today's Misspelling, Tomorrow's Dictionary Entry

Resistance is futile. We will add your biological and technological distinctiveness to our own. Your culture will adapt to service ours.
—THE BORG, from "Star Trek: The Next Generation"

*I*n the "Star Trek" universe of the future, the Borg collective is a technological hive—a race of dehumanized cyborgs who, in their box-shaped space vessels, exist solely to perfect their technology. The Borg message to humans is elegant in its simplicity: "Prepare to be assimilated."

Perhaps the assimilation has already begun, but in our box-like dwellings and cubicles rather than light-years away.

Long have humans feared that technology is little by little taking away our individuality and humanness—an unstoppable force that advances regardless of whether we cooperate or resist. In terms of modern popular culture, the Borg collective is, with the possible exception of Darth Vader, one of the most potent symbols of this fear. However, you can trace the essence of this anxiety to ancient myths such as the Greek tale of Icarus, whose "scientist" father created artificial wings so the boy could soar with the gods. Despite his father's warning, Icarus flew too high and close to the sun god, and Icarus plummeted to his death when the wings melted. Technology has always been thus for humans—offering the ability to go beyond our mortal limits, while also bringing new ways for us to perish when we venture too far from these limits.

More than once within these pages, I have lamented how we increasingly depend on technology to correct misspellings when we should be improving our spelling ability. So I will say no more on this point except this: spell-checkers alone will neither melt wings nor transform your neighbor into a cyborg, but neither will spell-checkers help us become linguistically fluent and capable—not unless we remember these are tools, not decision makers.

Misspellings as Independence

Let's complicate the matter. I have argued we should improve our spelling skills to be independent of the machine. Nonetheless, misspellings can be a useful tool for signifying independence, protest, and nonconformity. Every rule will be broken to make a point, and this principle applies to spelling.

Before looking at clear examples of this notion, we should consider a more subtle relationship between spelling and independence. All rules will also be broken while people are learning how to follow them.

Each of us has misspelled while attending to something more important—such as learning to spell. We cannot learn without making a mistake. Young children learning to spell go through identifiable stages during which they are consciously and subconsciously testing many hypotheses about spelling (along with grammar and word choice). The term "creative spelling" is frequently applied to the way a first grader might spell *dog* as *dawg* or *are* as *ar*. Unfortunately, this term has become a lightning rod for critics who assume it means teachers are interested *only* in warm and fuzzy concepts such as empowerment and self-esteem. Some teachers no doubt ignore all aspects of spelling in hopes students will focus on artistic expression, but relatively few teachers go to this extreme. If young children become too focused on getting each and every spelling correct, then they will do what most adults would do— avoid learning new words, use only the safest of spellings, and write as little as possible. The overwhelming majority of teachers who appreciate the concept of creative spelling fully understand a student must learn to spell correctly, but most also realize creative spellings can be a sign of learning and must be graded, corrected, and read with a degree of tolerance and understanding of the learning process.

Misspellings are just as natural as the act of spelling correctly. The only person who has never misspelled a word is someone never given the opportunity to become literate. Certainly, we all err in spellings as we experiment and learn new words, but by the time we are adults, we should have progressed beyond the developmental stages of our early years when creative spellings were the hallmark, rather than the exception, of our ways of spelling.

When people are first learning to spell, their misspellings tend to reflect how they are trying to reconcile social conventions for spelling with their own ideas of how a word should logically be spelled. In the previous chapter, I noted how Henry Thoreau realized that writers obediently follow rules even when it is foolish to do so. Whether it is a rule on using prepositions or spelling *transcendentalism*, all rules for Standard English come down to making us conform, to adhere to how other people want us to talk or write. Such conformity usually helps us communicate more effectively. Imagine reading the newspaper if each journalist were allowed to use whatever spellings he or she preferred that day. Still, there is no denying our spelling conventions are also sending a message not unlike what a Borg might offer: "Your preferences are irrelevant. You will conform. Prepare for your spellings to be assimilated and transformed."

Young children might not consciously understand they are "bucking the system" when they misspell, but in other social situations, misspellings reflect a deliberate attempt to get attention, be individualistic, bond with fellow nonconformists, or protest against "the man" (whom we might assume to be, in a symbolic way, Noah Webster). I have discussed the deliberate use of faulty spellings in advertisements, but consider other forms of intentional misspellings. Whether these are effective or not in reaching the authors' goals, we can still learn a great deal about the nature and significance of spelling by understanding why people would create this most heinous act of illiteracy—the deliberate, blatant misspelling.

Misspellings can provide ties that bind. Much earlier in this book, I spoke unkindly of the profusion of abbreviations on the Internet and in various modes of technological communication. These grow largely out of inordinate casualness, negligence, and lethargy, but abbreviations also result from fast-paced schedules laden with multitasking. We can detect yet another dimension to these language choices: with young people in particular, these odd wordings, abbreviations, and spellings help create a community or subculture that wants the world to know the conventions and rules of larger society— symbolized by Standard English—are not for everyone. These attitudes and goals are nothing new. Adolescents in particular have always found a way to use language in ways that shock and attempt to exclude an older generation, whether the language involves pig Latin or street talk.

Electronic communication is replete with misspellings (and I include most unconventional abbreviations as borderline misspellings), and many of these help establish a subculture or a group identity. The problem is we are still at the threshold of this phenomenon in electronics, so the conventions of these sub-cultures are still being created and defined. People do not agree on the names given to the dialects or language varieties we find on the Internet and elsewhere — *txtspk, technospeak, webspeak,* and *geekspeak* are just four examples of terms sometimes seen as equivalent, sometimes seen as different. The names are still being defined, as are the spellings commonly used within these systems. Two of the more identifiable genres are leetspeak and gamespeak, both heavily dependent on intentional misspellings.

As with most other varieties of technological communica-tion, leetspeak is primarily found in instant messages (IMs), online gaming, chat rooms, and cell phone text messages. True leetspeak is found in writing, not speech, despite the name. The term stands for "elite speak," suggesting how this language vari-ety belongs not only to a particular subgroup but to one that is better than conventional society or groups of newbies, also known as "n00bs" (people who are new to a technological cul-ture or forum). This ironic notion that nonstandard spellings, rather than standard ones, can be used to discriminate is an important point I will return to shortly.

Leetspeek utilizes any letter, number, or symbol found on the keyboard, but numbers play a particularly important role. They typically replace letters that appear similar, as with *3* standing for *E*. For instance, *leetspeak* itself could be spelled *133t5p33k* or even *!337$p34k*. As those examples show, leetspeak is usually not a matter of being concise but a matter of making communication difficult unless you are an "insider"—a mem-ber of this elite group. Other examples include *2m0r0* (*tomor-row*), *h4xx* (*hack,* as in trying to cheat or disrupt a program), *rox0rz* (*rocks,* as in "She rocks"), and *ph34r* (*fear,* with *ph* stand-ing for *f* to make the message even more cryptic). Because the spellings are meant to be cryptic and elitist, they are particu-larly subject to change and variation, for once "outsiders" figure out the meaning of, say, *rox0rz*, it is definitely uncool to use that spelling.

Gamespeak is used almost exclusively during online gaming, especially with MMORGs ("massively multiplayer online role-playing game") when dozens of players communicate with each other about a game they are currently playing. Increasingly, a message can be given through actual speech using a headset, but keyboard communication will likely remain a primary mode for gamespeak. Given the gaming context, the spellings reflect words, phrases, and emotions found in situations that tend to be highly competitive and dominated by young males. Indeed, the language of gamespeak helps create not merely "groups" but "alliances" or "clans"—gamers who unite to share resources and strategies, as well as to provide mutual protection when playing online.

Unlike leetspeak, gamespeak focuses on expeditiously conveying information. After all, the gamers might be dodging swords or wielding weapons of mass destruction. Because profanity can lead to being booted from a MMORG, gamespeak is also used to disguise swearing. Examples of gamespeak include *w00t* ("we own the other team") and *STFU* ("shut the f*** up"). The most interesting example is *pwn*, which means "to dominate an opponent" in an online game. According to most theories, the term originated as a common typographical error: *pwn* for *own* (the letters are close together on a keyboard). It is not unusual for typographical misspellings to be embraced by gamers or other individuals using electronic communication. Several keyboard slips that have resulted in widespread acceptance among the initiated include *pron* (*porn*), *aer* (*are*), *liek* (*like*), and *teh* (*the*). The nuances in the meaning of such terms vary. At times they can be used to convey sarcasm and contempt for the reader's intelligence or gaming skills. An experienced gamer might use *ehlp* (*help*) as a way of making fun of a less experienced gamer who is seeking assistance and prob-ably unaware of the connotations of the veteran player's "typo."

Online and offline, deliberate misspellings can reflect the writer's desire to be different or stylish. What I call "cute" mis-spellings fall into this category. In many contexts we can find intentional misspellings such as *kewl* (*cool*), *kasual* (*casual*), *dood* (*dude*), and *wut* (*what*), although one could argue the final exam-ple is intended to help the user save time by preventing one keystroke.

A similar type of cute spelling has increasingly been affect-ing children whose well-meaning parents want their progeny to stand out as being different and special. The trend, which seems to affect the naming of females more than males, has been especially apparent in America, giving rise to names such as *Linzee*, *Aimee*, and *Brandyn* (as opposed to humdrum *Lind-say*, *Amy*, and *Brandon*). The Institute for Naming Children Humanely argues that this approach to naming babies is a dis-service rather than an asset. If it takes a mere five seconds for Linzee to correct someone's spelling of her name, the institute estimates a grand total of fifty-eight days of Linzee's life will be spent on helping people spell her name. Perhaps, then, this method of providing an adorable name should be reserved for the naming of pets, for it is unlikely the issue will consume any of their precious cat and dog years.

Writers might purposely misspell in order to test hypothe-ses about spellings, express individuality, obfuscate meaning, or establish a group identity. Intentional misspellings can also have a more consciousness-raising intent or political edge. That is, they can make us think about social issues that are reflected in the way we spell.

Consider the way in which advocates for women's rights have demonstrated time and time again how "proper English" reflects and helps maintain inequalities between men and women. As Dale Spender puts it in her book *Man Made Language*: "Language is not neutral. It is not merely a vehicle which carries ideas. It is itself a shaper of ideas." Nowhere is this seen more clearly than with what English teachers once called the "generic *he*": the use of *he*, *him*, and *his* as supposedly including both males and females, as in "A doctor should respect his patients." Research has shown that people—especially young girls—frequently do not feel included in such uses of the third-person masculine pronouns.

The genderized nature of language does not always take such blatant forms. You might not agree with some of the arguments or alleged examples of patriarchal spellings, but feminist respellings do meet their goals of making people think about these important issues.

The words *woman* and *women* are prime examples. For some people, the spellings imply females are a subcategory of men. For others, changing the spelling to *womyn, wimyn, womin*, or *wimmin* offers females a symbolic way to redefine themselves as being distinct from males—as being able to describe themselves in their own terms. As with any neologism, the meanings of these feminine revisions of spelling are not altogether clear or consistent. Other revised spellings include *herstory, mynstruate*, and *humyn*. A person might use these spellings without intending to change the original meaning. However, when deliberately altering the spelling, the connation and meaning can change as well. For instance, in changing *theology* to *thealogy*, the emphasis is shifted to feminine issues within the study of religion (*thea-* in *theology* is derived from the name of the Greek goddess Thea).

Given the deliberate intent to use spellings that communicate a particular meaning and connotation, many revised spellings seem more akin to alternative spellings than misspellings. They might be "errors" in the sense they do not adhere to standard conventions of English, but a spelling such as *wimmin* is not made erroneously—the term achieves its effect regardless of whether a reader approves of the spelling or not. Poets, songwriters, and other artists have long used alternative spellings to convey a sense of rebellion against social standardization. Sometimes, in fact, the more negative a reaction is, the more some people might consider the respelling a success in making readers attend to issues of gender and language.

Standard spellings do facilitate communication, but like any other rule that determines what is deemed correct and proper, spelling has an elitist dimension. Spelling can be used unfairly to discriminate between the "haves and have-nots"—between, for instance, those who are considered educated and those who are not. As noted in the first chapter of this book, I believe humans are bound to be elitist in terms of language, given the centrality of language to defining our individual lives as well as the human race. People are elitist not merely about Standard English but about all varieties of this language. Depending on your readers, you might be considered a patriarchal "outsider" or a pathetic "newbie" if you use *women* rather than *womyn* or use *leetspeak* for *133t5p33k*.

On one hand, I agree we should be less judgmental of people who do not use spellings we prefer, whether they be alternative or conventional spellings. On the other hand, our linguistic elitism will never vanish completely as long as we are a language-manipulating animal, so one reason I have written this book is to encourage people to be well prepared for elitist reactions to misspellings. The best way to be prepared is to improve our spelling skills and understandings of the complex history and nature of our orthographic system.

On Words and Onward

The English language is changing, just as it always has. The forces of change today are not sword-wielding Angles, Saxons, or Scandinavians. In the twenty-first century, technology, along with changing demographics, is bringing new spellings, words, and ideas into English.

The orthography of American English reminds me of its geography—a vast landscape of diversity, united and tamed by people who eventually found how much they have in common. To some people, it might seem as though the familiar coastline of American orthography is being both eroded and refashioned, bit by bit and word by word, by a disorderly ocean teeming with letters and sounds randomly deposited on our shores. However, I see this process of linguistic change as just another way in which our language is becoming increasingly flexible and durable—continuously restocked with new meanings, word choices, and spellings that offer us more possibilities for growth and cooperation.

English is increasingly becoming a global language, but as history has shown us, a "conquering" language is itself transformed in the process of being used and adopted by other cultures. Standard English is bound to change as global societies and cultures evolve. Indeed, the only language that ceases to change is a dead language such as Latin, which is no longer the native language of any culture. If you ever discern that English is no longer changing, you should assume we have bigger problems to worry about than correct spelling.

So let us move onward, toward growth rather than stagnation. But what is the future of American orthography? Some language experts have suggested that technological communication, such as e-mail and instant messages, are slowly but surely undermining the perception that we can have—or need—standards for spelling, grammar, and punctuation.

I disagree. Although it might have taken centuries for people to appreciate the value of standardizing English, it is now too firmly implanted for us to embrace the chaos of communication that forsakes consistency and clarity in favor of the expediency and ease of having no rules or conventions. Surely, our emerging modes and tools for communication will affect English, at the very least by offering new words and revised spellings. We will also see increasing informality in casual text messaging, e-mails, and whatever new modes of communication might develop next week. However, none of this means we will abandon a basic principle of language: communication requires clarity, and clarity requires having linguistic rules and widely accepted conventions allowing diverse individuals to understand one another.

English orthography, despite its amazing faults and irregularities, provides such rules and conventions. While I do not expect to live to see a major overhaul of this system, natural forces of linguistic evolution will create gradual changes, most of which should be improvements. Some changes, despite our lamentations, will take the form of embracing alternative spellings or accepting idiosyncratic spellings of slang words and neologisms.

Today's misspellings might indeed become tomorrow's dictionary entries—just as yesterday's rebels and nonconformists have frequently become today's business, religious, and political leaders.

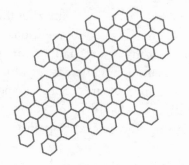

Bibliography

To understand spelling, we must tackle many facets of the English language, not to mention history, sociology, and philosophy. Listed here are major works I have drawn upon or recommend to readers wanting more detail on various issues covered in these pages.

Ball, Rodney. "Spelling Reform in France and Germany: Attitudes and Reactions." *Current Issues in Language and Society*, Vol. 6, No. 3 & 4, 1999.

Beason, Larry. "Ethos and Error: How Business People React to Errors." *College Composition and Communication*, Vol. 53, No. 1, 2001.

Cleary, Linda Miller, and Michael Linn. *Linguistics for Teachers*. New York: McGraw-Hill, Inc. 1993.

Connors, Robert, and Andrea Lunsford. "Exorcising Demonolatry: Spelling Patterns and Pedagogy in College Writing." *Written Communication*, Vol. 9, No. 3, 1992.

Fisher, John. *The Emergence of Standard English*. Lexington, KY: University Press of Kentucky, 1996.

Fitzgerald, James. *The Teaching of Spelling*. Milwaukee: Bruce Publishing, 1951.

Gaur, Albertine. *A History of Writing*. New York: Cross River Press, 1992.

Holmes, Virginia, and Anne Castles. "Unexpectedly Poor Spelling in University Students." *Scientific Studies of Reading*, Vol. 5, No. 3, 2001.

Johnston, Francine. "Spelling Exceptions: Problems or Possibilities?" *Reading Teacher*, Vol. 4, No. 4, 2001.

Jones, John, Brett Pelham, Mauricio Carvallo, and Matthew Mirenberg. "How Do I Love Thee? Let Me Count the Js: Implicit Egotism and Interpersonal Attraction." *Journal of Personality and Social Psychology*, Vol. 87, No. 5, 2004.

Kessler, Brett, and Rebecca Treiman. "Is English Spelling Chaotic? Misconceptions Concerning Its Irregularity." *Reading Psychology*, Vol. 24, No. 3 & 4, 2003.

Kreidler, Charles. "Noah Webster's Linguistic Influences." *Language and Communication*, Vol. 18, No. 2, 1998.

Labov, William. *Principles of Linguistic Change: Internal Factors*. Oxford: Blackwell Publishers, 1994.

MacDonald, G. Wayne, and Anne Cornwall. "The Relationship Between Phonological Awareness and Reading and Spelling Achievement: Eleven Years Later." *Journal of Learning Disabilities*, Vol. 28, No. 8, 1995.

Man, John. Alpha Beta: *How 26 Letters Shaped the Western World*. New York: Barnes & Noble Books, 2000.

McCrum, Robert, William Cran, and Robert MacNeil. *The Story of English*. New York: Elisabeth Sifton Books, 1986.

Pinker, Stephen. *The Language Instinct: How the Mind Creates Language*. William Morrow & Co., 1994.

Pyles, Thomas, and John Algeo. *The Origins and Development of the English Language*, 5th edition. Boston: Heinle Press, 2004.

Ranow, George. "Simplified Spelling in Government Publications." *American Speech*, Vol. 29, No. 1, 1954.

Scragg, D. G. *A History of English Spelling*. Manchester: Manchester University Press, 1974.

Seymor, Philip, Mikko Aro, and Jane Erskine. "Foundation Literacy Acquisition in European Orthographies." *British Journal of Psychology*, Vol. 94, No. 2, 2003.

Templeton, Shane, and Darrell Morris. "Questions Teachers Ask About Spelling." *Reading Research Quarterly*, Vol. 34, No. 1, 1999.

Treiman, Rebecca. "Spelling and Dialect: Comparisons Between Speakers of African American Vernacular English and White Speakers." *Psychonomic Review*, Vol. 11, No. 2, 2002.

Treiman, Rebecca, and Derrick Bourassa. "The Development of Spelling Skill." *Topics in Language Disorders*, Vol. 20, No. 3, 2000.

Treiman, Rebecca, Brett Kessler, and Suzanne Bick. "Context Sensitivity in the Spelling of English Vowels." *Journal of Memory and Language*, Vol. 47, No. 3, 2002.

Venezky, Richard. *The Structure of English Orthography*. The Hague: Mouton & Co., 1970.

Venezky, Richard. *The American Way of Spelling: The Structure and Origins of American English Orthography*. New York: Guilford Press, 1999.

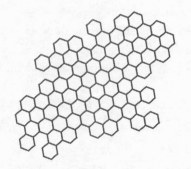

Index